Work Well.
Live Well.

The Remote Workers' Guide to Productivity, Well-Being and Personal Growth in the Modern Workspace

Andreja Borin

Work Well. Live Well.
The Remote Workers' Guide to Productivity, Well-being, and Personal Growth in the Modern Workspace
Copyright © 2025 by Andreja Borin

ISBN: 9781068365904 Paperback

Published by: Inspired By Publishing

Dedication

To my nurturing family and soulful friends, who journey with me and remind me that I belong, that I am loved, that I am light.

To all who brought challenges to my path – thank you for unveiling my inner wisdom, resilience and determination.

Acknowledgements

First, to my family and friends – thank you for your unwavering belief, love and support. Your encouragement and trust in my potential made this book possible. Your presence has been the quiet strength behind each word on these pages.

To the individuals I have had the privilege to lead, those who have led and guided me, and those whose leadership I have admired from afar – thank you. Your resilience, vision and commitment have continuously inspired me and profoundly shaped my journey. Each of you has been a guide, motivating me to explore deeper and reach further. For this, I am deeply grateful.

I extend my heartfelt gratitude to three luminaries who have illuminated my path and empowered my growth: Bette Jo Toppin, LMHC—a beautiful soul sister and therapist who has loved me through every version of myself. Your brilliance and compassion have been invaluable, shaping my professional growth and personal evolution; Professor Felice Bedford at the University of Arizona, whose insightful work and support provided the foundation for a significant transformation in my life; and Deb Dana, whose work and training in Polyvagal Theory continues to guide me towards becoming the person and psychologist I have long aspired to be. You each shine as true beacons, touching lives with empowerment and kindness.

To everyone who has touched my life on this journey – mentors, colleagues, and readers – it has been an honour to connect with you. Each of you has left an indelible mark, shaping me into a better human being. Thank you for contributing in your unique way to my growth and evolution.

Contents

Introduction

Wellness in the workplace should be a foundational, not optional, part of professional life. Over the years, I have worked with diverse clients – from high-performing athletes fine-tuning their bodies for peak performance to office workers grappling with the pains of poor ergonomics and the weight of stress. Time and again, I have witnessed how small, informed adjustments can create enormous benefits, transforming how people work and how they feel about their lives as a whole. These changes aren't about perfection or quick fixes; they are sustainable shifts that ripple outward, improving energy, focus and your sense of balance and well-being. When these shifts take hold, they bring clarity and stability to even the most demanding days, creating a foundation for long-term fulfilment and success.

Imagine stepping into your workday not with the usual feelings of sluggishness, stress or fatigue but with a vibrant sense of calm, resilience and purpose. This vision might seem unattainable in a world where the boundaries between work and personal life have blurred, and professionals are constantly adapting to hybrid or remote work models. Yet, it is entirely within reach when you approach your day equipped with the tools and knowledge of physical, emotional and mental well-being. A startling statistic highlights why this is so important: Studies show that 77% of working adults experience physical symptoms caused by chronic stress, with over 55% reporting difficulties maintaining work-life balance and health in remote setups.[1] For many, these challenges feel overwhelming and inescapable. That is why this book was created – for you, the professional navigating these pressures. It is here to show that a life infused with purpose, mindful productivity and well-being is possible and achievable, no matter your work environment or personal constraints.

Whether it is creating an ergonomic workspace that supports your body, embracing a nourishing meal plan to fuel your energy, prioritising restorative sleep to refresh your mind and spirit, engaging in mindful movement to stay active and grounded, or rediscovering the joy of intentional play, these practices can unlock new levels of fulfilment and success. They aren't about dramatic overhauls but small, meaningful changes that add to transformative results. This book will explore the essential aspects of well-being and productivity, bridging complex but often overlooked concepts with your daily routines and professional growth. From ergonomics to nutrition, mindfulness to polyvagal theory, and sleep to movement, each chapter builds on the last to offer a practical and holistic approach that integrates seamlessly into your lifestyle.

Here is what you will gain:

- **Awareness and understanding** of the physiological and psychological factors impacting your productivity and health. Concepts like polyvagal theory, mindfulness and play are not just theoretical; they can reshape how you manage stress, achieve balance and remain grounded.

- **Practical tools and strategies** to address modern challenges, from remote work ergonomics to time management for business travellers. These tools, grounded in current research, including neuroscience and behavioural studies, empower you to make informed, effective decisions.

- **A blueprint for sustainable growth** with actionable insights into goal-setting, career development, and holistic well-being encompassing nutrition, restorative sleep, mindful movement, breathwork and optimised ergonomics. These strategies will enhance your performance and support long-term health, transforming your approach to work and life.

The need for a balanced, healthy approach to work has never been greater. Remote and hybrid work models, while flexible, introduce a range of unique challenges: increased sedentary behaviour, feelings of isolation, blurred boundaries between work and personal life, the strain of poor posture from makeshift workspace setups and the constant pressure to remain "always on" in a digitally connected world. A study by the National Bureau of Economic Research reveals that the average workday for remote workers has been extended by nearly 48 minutes, often with detrimental effects on health, mental well-being and job satisfaction.[2] These challenges are not just personal; they ripple into professional performance and organisational success. The stakes are high. Poor mental health and physical stressors among employees cost the global economy up to $1 trillion annually in lost productivity.[3] Whether you are an individual seeking more balance or a leader aiming to create healthier, more engaged teams, the tools and strategies in this book are designed to help you navigate and thrive in these evolving professional landscapes.

Why is now the right time to make these changes? Because waiting only compounds the issues. Left unaddressed, chronic stress, physical discomfort and unhealthy habits lead to burn-out, reduced productivity and long-term health challenges. Yet, with the right knowledge and small, intentional steps, these obstacles can become opportunities for growth and resilience. This book equips you with the tools to do just that.

This journey isn't about quick fixes or surface-level solutions. It is about creating sustainable, meaningful change and trans-forming how you approach work and life. You can achieve pro-fessional success and find harmony within yourself, allowing success to flow naturally from a place of authentic connection and balance. Remember, real change requires effort and en-gagement. Throughout this book, you will be guided through reflections and exercises to connect deeply with your goals and values. The process will ask for your commitment because no one else can make these changes for you. When you honour your well-being, you don't just work better – you live better. And that is where the real transformation begins. This belief drives everything I do and has shaped the heart of this book. Let us start this journey together if you are ready to unlock a more vibrant, resilient, and connected version of yourself.

Chapter 1
Transitioning to Remote Work

"Change the way you look at things and
the things you look at change."
– Wayne Dyer

The pandemic was a global event that affected us all on a personal level. The world has moved on since then, and the landscape has become different. We as people have changed, along with our communities, work environments and approaches to social interaction. The work structure, especially, has changed, whether it was your choice to transition to remote work or you found yourself mandated to work from home due to the pandemic and had to adapt to the circumstances.

New opportunities and perspectives have also emerged, such as the rise of remote work and digital transformation, as well as a greater emphasis on mental health. Investment into self-development and self-care has become more prominent, alongside challenges like economic uncertainty and adapting to rapidly evolving technologies. All these elements now shape our personal journeys and influence how we navigate life. As we face economic uncertainties and rapidly evolving technologies, we are called to be more adaptable, resilient and mindful of our well-being. These shifts are not merely changes in our work structure or environment; they are catalysts that push us to reassess our values, redefine our goals and refine our daily routines. They invite us to create a life that aligns more closely with who we are becoming, helping us grow with purpose and intention. The pandemic has taught us that the human system is not merely individual; rather, it is an individual functioning within a broader system. Collective cohesion, therefore, begins with each of us.

To start, transitioning from a traditional office environment to remote work, whether part-time or full-time, is a significant shift that requires some consideration and planning. When people come to know that I work remotely and from home, they oftentimes glamorise it by thinking that I vacation full-time. The truth is – I, too, thought I would have more time for "fun stuff" when I started my business, and I had to learn lessons the hard way. The idea of freedom and being your own boss is tempting, but it requires hard and dedicated work.

Now, I would not change it for anything. However, you do need to work on yourself and be open to change and learning opportunities. The initial phase and change are the most challenging, but once you create the system that works for you and aligns with your values, you'll start to recognise the person you want to become. Once you feel content and balanced, your rhythm is in flow – you'll know then that every effort was worth it. Every change, no matter how small, has been transforming your life. This is called continuous growth.

Understanding this transition begins with acknowledging the shifts in work dynamics, communication methods and daily habits – all of which evolve, taking on new shapes and forms. You might need to adapt, learn new skills and seek additional resources and support. The initial phase often involves adjusting to the absence of a structured office environment and the spontaneous interactions that come with it.

This shift requires you to independently create a remote work routine, ensuring it aligns with the results you want to achieve. Often, this journey involves learning by trial and error until you establish the routines and boundaries that suit you best. This process unfolds organically and requires full engagement to build a strong foundation for long-term success. To navigate it effectively, you must be open to change, starting with yourself. It begins with acknowledging the need for transformation and then taking proactive steps to make it happen, embracing the growth that comes with each adjustment.

Don't be discouraged if you face challenges. These moments will test you, push you to grow and strengthen your resilience. This is your opportunity to refine your approach: Experiment with routines, test different strategies and see what truly aligns with your goals and values. Allow yourself the space to explore, experiment and adapt as you discover the rhythms and routines that support your unique needs and aspirations. This journey is as much about self-discovery as it is about building an effective work-life structure. For me, what began as simply building a business has evolved into a lifestyle. I no longer see it as work; I see it as an outlet for creative expression, creation and development – something I genuinely enjoy. This view is often true for many entrepreneurs, where passion and purpose intertwine, transforming their work into a meaningful and fulfilling way of life.

During this transition, you are now also responsible for actively maintaining your professional relationships and personal connections. It is important to check in with yourself regularly and set realistic expectations about time management during this period. When planning your time, consider your workload and productivity, the quality time spent with family and friends, and the time dedicated to your well-being. Self-care often takes a back seat, but it should be a priority because, without sufficient energy for yourself, you may experience burnout, which will lead to significant personal and professional challenges.

Equally important is surrounding yourself with friends who genuinely believe in you, are honest and are willing to give you a reality check if you go astray. These people genuinely want to see you succeed and offer constructive criticism because they have your best interests at heart. You may notice some people gradually fading from your life as your standards, values and boundaries evolve. This isn't a loss but a natural progression, a sign that you align more closely with people who support your growth and share your vision for a fulfilling, authentic life.

I encourage you to reflect on the proactive steps you have taken in your transition to remote work. What insights or feelings come up for you? Feel free to journal your thoughts; writing them down can provide clarity and help you process your experiences more deeply.

One of the key reasons I am writing this book is that living through and beyond the pandemic has placed immense stress on our nervous systems. This global event was a collective experience, yet it impacted each of us on a deeply personal level.

Take a moment to reflect – when you were suddenly forced to change your work routine under such stress and uncertainty, did you truly consider the importance of ergonomics, self-care, nutrition or even sleep quality? Or was your mind consumed with worry? Worry for your family, children, relatives and friends? How did your nervous system respond to these overwhelming stressors? Did you notice changes in your energy levels, focus or emotional resilience? Many people lost their jobs, changed careers, relocated and experienced significant life changes. During the lockdowns, people experienced prolonged isolation, leading many to face challenges with re-entering social networks and rebuilding connections. Until now, many are still dealing with the consequences of the pandemic. It is worth reflecting on how these factors have shaped your journey since then and how they continue influencing your daily life.

This constant state of concern often overshadowed the need to prioritise our well-being, leaving many of us struggling to find a balance between adapting to new work environments and maintaining our mental and physical health. Fast forward to 2025, and many are still grappling with the aftermath, only now beginning to fully grasp its profound impact on their systems. This may be a natural response to an unnatural situation. While your nervous system was attempting to process and regulate the stress of the pandemic, the underlying events continued to unfold, often quietly exerting their effects long after the initial crisis passed. The delayed impact is only now coming to light for many as the body and mind slowly emerge from survival mode.

So, we ask ourselves: How do I navigate my current circumstances with greater awareness now that more resources and understanding are available? How can I consciously rebuild and nurture my well-being, integrating the lessons learned from this collective experience into a more resilient and balanced life?

Office-Based Employment vs Remote Work Arrangements

Traditional office-based and remote work has unique advantages and challenges, affecting people differently. For some, working in a traditional office environment has always meant directly communicating with colleagues, receiving immediate feedback and enjoying easier collaboration. These aspects have undoubtedly contributed to strong team cohesion and encouraged a vibrant corporate culture that many value. Traditional office environments offer the benefit of direct, face-to-face communication, where body language and nonverbal cues improve understanding and encourage stronger interpersonal connections.

These subtle forms of communication are important for effective teamwork, as they help convey emotions, build trust and create a sense of cohesion among team members.[1] The physical presence in an office setting can significantly contribute to a company's culture and collaboration efforts, enabling spontaneous interactions that can lead to creative problem-solving and innovation. If you hold a leadership position within the firm, your team also needs to feel your presence.

While hybrid work offers flexibility, your physical presence is essential and non-negotiable. Your team relies on you for support, guidance and leadership, and being present in the office strengthens a sense of connection and trust that is vital for their well-being and the organisation's overall success.

There is also a profound level of intimacy and connection that comes from seeing people in person, which virtual relationships cannot replace. Physical touch, for instance, is a fundamental aspect of human nature and development, playing an important role in our emotional and social well-being.[2] However, during and after the pandemic, physical touch became something our nervous systems were conditioned to perceive as a threat, a source of danger and infection.

This shift in perception has profoundly impacted our interactions and relationships, leading many to keep their distance instinctively. Losing this fundamental human interaction highlights our unique challenges in maintaining genuine connections in a predominantly virtual world.

Without the comfort of physical presence, we must navigate new ways to build trust, warmth and intimacy in our relationships, reminding ourselves of the essential human need for closeness and connection.

"When you touch the skin, it stimulates pressure sensors under the skin that send messages to the vagus (a nerve in the brain). As vagal activity increases, the nervous system slows down, heart rate and blood pressure decrease and your brain waves show relaxation. Levels of stress hormones such as cortisol are also decreased."
– Tiffany Field

Online coaching, for instance, was initially challenging for me, both as a client and as a coach, as well as during other virtual meetings. Having always been "old school" in my approach to interactions, it took time to acclimate to this new mode of virtual engagement and to build genuine rapport. I recall being overly conscientious of my body language, constantly aware of how I appeared on screen while speaking. This focus on the forensics of my appearance often pulled me out of the present moment, disrupting the connection I was trying to establish. This dissonance showed a lack of congruency between my body language and verbal communication.

Recognising this, I knew I had to change my approach. Now, I prepare before virtual meetings, centring myself to ensure I am fully present and aligned in my communication. I learned to observe myself and acknowledge the misalignment of energies within me, embracing the need to be teachable, to listen, learn and continue to improve and grow.

Additionally, I am a hugger by nature – I deeply value the warmth of a genuine hug. It is a beautiful exchange of energy, a way to physically feel the presence and closeness of another human being, and a powerful sign of support, compassion and connection. Affectionate touch, such as hugs, has been shown to lower cortisol levels[3] and increase oxytocin, promoting less stress and more joy. This tactile connection, which we all once took for granted, is something I have come to appreciate even more in our increasingly virtual world. So, whenever you can, hug your loved ones – embrace those moments of closeness, warmth and presence that remind us of our shared humanity and offer a grounding reminder of the beauty of real connection. In a world where distance is often the norm, these moments of touch are anchors that keep us connected to each other and to what truly matters.

As we recognise the value of in-person connections, we are also re-evaluating the traditional office setup and the toll it often takes on our well-being. While the office provides camaraderie and collaboration, it also comes with challenges that many are now questioning.

Have the long commutes often left you feeling drained before the workday even begins? Do rigid schedules sometimes make finding a healthy balance between work commitments and personal life challenging? Have you felt like you have been on autopilot for quite some time now, unable to catch up with sleep or do any exercises? Often, you may find yourself taking work home just to catch up, blurring the lines between work and personal time and leading to increased stress and burnout.

As much as one can appreciate the camaraderie and energy of the office, many have longed for more flexibility and autonomy in how they structure their workdays. After all, a more flexible schedule can lead to improved work-life balance, reduced stress and increased job satisfaction.

Remote work offers precisely that: greater flexibility, reduced commuting time, and potentially a better synergy between work and life. In fact, many remote workers report feeling more productive and experiencing improved work-life balance. However, they also face challenges, such as feelings of isolation and the need for self-discipline. While remote work offers clear advantages, like flexible hours and the freedom to choose your workspace, these benefits come with challenges that require mindful management.

With the time saved from commuting, many people find they can dedicate more attention to activities that previously felt out of reach. Some of my clients have used this extra time to connect with their families, prioritise fitness or focus on nutrition by preparing meals at home. Others have taken it as an opportunity for self-development, enrolling in courses and training to grow personally and professionally.

Remote work also allows space to explore passions, whether learning new skills, engaging in community or cultural activities, volunteering or even exploring ways to create passive income or start a side business. The possibilities are endless, and it is about finding what truly lights you up and aligns with your values.

By tapping into this newfound flexibility, remote work can become more than just a way of earning a living – it can be a pathway to personal growth and fulfilment.

Reflecting on this section, what thoughts arise for you? Take a moment to note activities, educational pursuits or any other desires you have wanted to pursue but have not had the time for. After writing them down, revisit the list and observe the emotions that surface. Do you feel excitement, envision new opportunities, experience happiness – or do you experience unease because you are uncertain how to navigate it all? Remember, there is no right or wrong answer here. If you feel uneasy and your nervous system is signalling discomfort, take a deep breath and relax. It is important to recognise that you are not alone when feeling overwhelmed. Remote work entails a heightened responsibility for managing time, making and executing decisions, and regulating behaviours.

I remember when I started my own business. Initially, I had a lot of free time during the day because I did fieldwork on some days and worked from my home office on other days. At first, I was excited about all the things I could do. I had plans to run the London marathon, go hiking, travel, improve my photography skills, learn languages, meditate, switch to a raw vegan diet, get a skydiving licence, see my friends more often, travel, and all of that on top of exploring different ways to make money with my business. I was enthusiastic, passionate and confident in my abilities. But as time passed, I realised I was not managing my time well. I started feeling frustrated because I was not getting things done, overwhelmed by all the tasks I had set for myself and guilty for not accomplishing them. I even started taking days off to try to get organised and spark creativity, but it did not help. I remember sitting in my garden one day and realising I was nowhere near where I wanted to be. I had not gone hiking even once, hurt my knee while training and could not run the marathon, had not touched my camera, wrote meditation scripts but had not recorded them, and had not gone skydiving. I was also ordering takeaway because "I did not have time to cook," which was out of character for me. It was clear that something needed to change. But how and what?

I began by focusing on three key aspects within my immediate control that directly affected my mental well-being: sleep, nutrition and physical activity. I also reflected on how effectively these elements worked together – or where they did not – to support my overall health.

Establishing consistency in these areas allowed other positive changes to fall into place. With improved mental clarity and energy, I gained a clearer vision of my business objectives. I found effective ways to structure my day for a sense of accomplishment, creativity, productivity and happiness. It is important to understand that this was not an instant fix. It was a gradual process of recognising and reshaping my habits and thought patterns to create new neural pathways and develop new behaviours. Remember, our brain has neuroplasticity, which means we can change its structure. However, this transformation is not instantaneous; it requires deliberate and consistent effort over time to truly embed these changes and endorse lasting growth.

Additionally, I reached out to Tom, aka Norx, a personal trainer and coach, who played an important role in helping me get back on track. As a former PT, I initially felt ashamed to ask for this support, but I soon realised that, no matter where you are in life, it is important to swallow your pride and learn to lean on others. Individuals like Tom genuinely want the best for you and are invested in seeing you succeed. You should surround yourself with these types of people – those who uplift you, support your growth and encourage you to reach your full potential.

The journey to healing is not straightforward. Sometimes, I doubted myself, felt frustrated and was alone. My mind often led me astray, triggering a cycle of negative emotions. But I kept trying. Each time, I learned more about myself and how my patterns affect my nervous system.

There will be days when you struggle to get out of bed, lack motivation, miss deadlines, feel tired or dread meetings. In those moments, be kind to yourself. Instead of judging, observe your experiences without criticism.

Listen to what your body tells you and understand your nervous system needs to feel better. Healing is about progress, not perfection, and each setback can be a chance to learn more about what truly nurtures you. Remember, the small, consistent acts of self-care create lasting change.

At the end of the day, the most important person you need to lead is yourself. You are your own leader, and each step forward is a testament to your strength.

The truth is remote work requires a strong mastery of self-discipline and time management. While it offers flexibility and can improve the balance between work and personal life, it also requires considerable effort to create the life you desire. This means sacrifice, commitment and continuous investment in yourself. It might mean staying in on weekends to work while your friends are out socialising, spending evenings researching or seeking mentorship instead of unwinding with Netflix, or waking up early to hit the gym while others are still asleep.

Building the life you envision often involves prioritising growth over immediate comfort, choosing focus over distraction and making intentional choices that align with your long-term goals – as you commit to establishing your routine, business or desired lifestyle.

This foundational phase may require you to make short-term sacrifices in exchange for the stability and freedom of a well-structured, purpose-driven life. Both employers and employees must navigate the benefits and challenges of traditional office work and remote work to encourage productive and fulfilling work environments in today's evolving landscape. Numerous stories show how individuals have successfully transitioned careers, discovered their true purpose and crafted the lives they envision. These examples are powerful reminders that transformative change is possible with the right mindset and effort.

The fundamental question is: Are you content with where you are now? What steps can you take to improve your well-being, creativity and productivity? How can you meet yourself where you are and refine your approach to elevate your personal and professional growth?

Establishing a Productive Mindset and Creating a Suitable Workspace at Home

A productive mindset and a well-organised workspace are important for successful remote work. Working towards a productive mindset includes setting clear goals, maintaining a routine, executing decisions with intention and leveraging productivity tools and techniques. Remote workers who establish a consistent daily routine often feel far more productive than those who don't. Some clients have shared that having a structure to their day helps them stay focused, motivated and on track with their tasks.

Creating a routine, even if flexible, provides stability and helps manage the blur between work and personal life that can sometimes happen when working remotely. A regular schedule and clear boundaries can significantly affect how you approach your work and maintain balance. Sometimes, your daily routine will be interrupted, throwing you off track. And that is okay. Accept it as part of the process and an opportunity to find alternative ways to manage the situation and understand what works best for you.

While you cannot control everything, you can become aware of how you respond to certain situations and create more flexibility to handle these shifts. You learn to channel your energy into the areas that sustain and support you.

Embracing a productive mindset goes beyond just having a routine; it is about cultivating a positive attitude, setting clear goals, managing time effectively and building resilience. This mindset also requires regular self-reflection and actively creating a supportive environment around you. Taking time to assess your progress, identify areas for improvement and celebrate small wins reinforces your commitment to growth.

Surrounding yourself with people, resources and habits that align with your goals strengthens motivation and helps you stay grounded, even when challenges arise. This intentional support system becomes the backbone of sustained productivity and resilience.

There are also specific techniques that can help keep you organised and reinforce a productive mindset, ensuring you stay focused and efficient throughout the day.

Setting SMART goals, managing priorities and breaking tasks into manageable intervals can help you maintain clarity and discipline over your workload. For example, setting specific, measurable, achievable, relevant and time-bound goals helps you stay focused and maintain a sense of clarity and direction throughout your day.

SMART GOALS

SPECIFIC

SMART GOALS

TIMED

MEASURABLE

RELEVANT

ACHIEVABLE

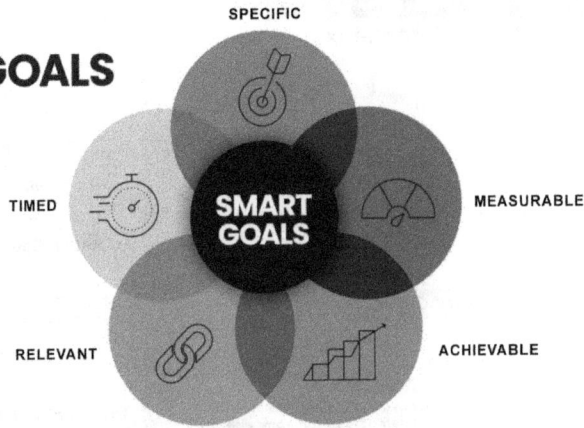

Knowing what you are working towards makes prioritising and avoiding feeling overwhelmed easier. Effective time management is key to making this happen.

Whether adjusting how you structure your day or finding new tools to help you stay on track, being creative and willing to stretch beyond your comfort zone can unlock even greater success.

Remember, you are intentionally breaking away from old patterns and purposefully creating new habits that align with the life you want to build. After all, it is in these small shifts in mindset and approach that real growth happens.

Eisenhower Matrix
Urgent-Important Matrix

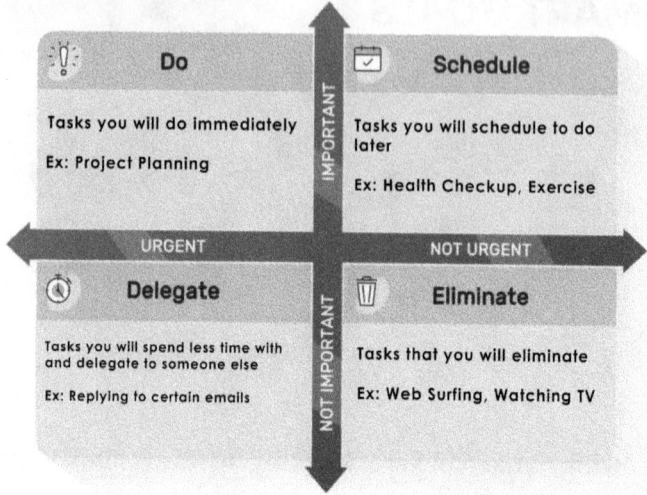

Do

Tasks you will do immediately

Ex: Project Planning

Schedule

Tasks you will schedule to do later

Ex: Health Checkup, Exercise

IMPORTANT

Delegate

Tasks you will spend less time with and delegate to someone else

Ex: Replying to certain emails

Eliminate

Tasks that you will eliminate

Ex: Web Surfing, Watching TV

NOT IMPORTANT

URGENT   NOT URGENT

A consistent routine doesn't just boost productivity; it also plays a vital role in your overall well-being, which is often over-looked in the hustle of daily life. It is easy to prioritise work and family, but if you are not caring for yourself, everything else eventually suffers.

Perhaps you have experienced burnout or felt stretched too thin, and it became clear that neglecting your needs impacted your ability to show up fully at work and in your personal life. It becomes much more challenging to effectively contribute to your job or support others around you without maintaining your well-being.

The **POMODORO** Technique

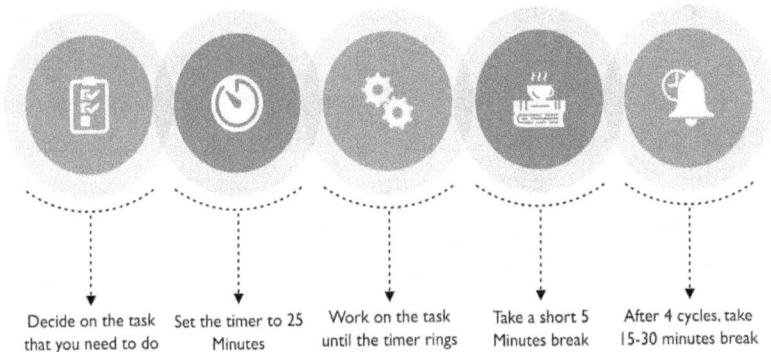

Decide on the task that you need to do	Set the timer to 25 Minutes	Work on the task until the timer rings	Take a short 5 Minutes break	After 4 cycles, take 15-30 minutes break

The good news is that self-care is within your immediate control, something you can practise anytime, anywhere, once you make it a priority. Self-care is about intentionally caring for your nervous system with calm and compassion in the present moment. This might mean taking time for mindful movement, deep breathing or simply giving yourself a moment to pause and reset.

Building self-care into your daily routine – whether through movement, mindfulness or even just taking a proper break for lunch – recharges your energy and focus. By nurturing your well-being, you create a solid foundation that allows your work, family and personal commitments to thrive. When you prioritise yourself with intention, everything else starts to fall into place more naturally, creating a ripple effect that benefits every area of your life.

"Taking care of yourself doesn't mean me first, it means me too."
– L.R. Knost

Embracing a productive mindset also means recognising the importance of balance. While it is essential to maintain focus and strive toward your goals, knowing when to slow down, rest or step back is equally important. Productivity isn't about constant hustle but working smarter, not just harder. Some clients have learned that pushing through without breaks often leads to burnout, reducing their overall effectiveness in the long run.

Knowing when to pause, recharge and give yourself time to rest is essential for sustaining your mental and physical energy. Taking breaks doesn't mean losing momentum; it allows you to return to your tasks with renewed focus and creativity. Rest is an essential part of the process, and recognising this balance can make all the difference in achieving long-term success. You learn to tune into your body and mind, recognising when to push forward and when to give yourself the grace to pause and recover.

I also encourage you to be playful and fully engage with the process. Remember, it is *you* that you are building – your growth, resilience and unique strengths. Enjoy the journey, understanding that while there will be challenges, each obstacle is an opportunity to grow stronger and more capable. At times, you may need to tap into deep resilience, but resilient individuals see setbacks as stepping stones for growth rather than insurmountable obstacles. They learn from hardships, applying those lessons to future endeavours, building a foundation of experience and wisdom. I would also like to add that growth is not just about financial success or reaching specific milestones; it is about evolving as both a person and a professional.

True success involves continuous personal development – learning new skills, expanding your emotional intelligence and refining the qualities that make you a better leader, partner or business professional. It is also about personal victories, like setting healthy boundaries, becoming more mindful of your nutrition and sleep or consistently showing up for yourself in ways that support your well-being.

Celebrate these achievements, whether completing a project, securing a new job, deepening your relationships or growing a skill. Every accomplishment, big or small, reflects the energy, commitment and effort you have invested in becoming a more fulfilled and capable version of yourself. Embrace and honour these victories, for they are the building blocks of the life and career you are shaping. *You* made them happen, and they are worth celebrating.

The most exciting – and at times challenging – aspect of personal growth you may experience is committing to regular self-reflection and mindfulness practices, both essential for developing and sustaining a productive mindset. These practices serve as steady anchors, helping you stay grounded, alleviate stress and maintain mental clarity amidst the demands of daily life. They are exciting because they provide moments of stillness, allowing you to observe your insights, become aware of your physical language and trust the unfolding process without rushing or forcing outcomes. Yet, this process can also be challenging, requiring you to step back intentionally, lean in and observe without distraction. These moments call for deep honesty with yourself, a willingness to avoid getting caught up in familiar narratives, and, instead, to witness patterns and conditioning without judgment in the present moment.

Over time, this commitment to self-reflection develops resilience, helping you build a foundation of self-awareness that enriches both personal and professional growth. The process may not always be easy, but it brings lasting rewards, teaching you to approach life with compassion, clarity and a stronger sense of purpose. Embracing this journey ultimately empowers you to lead with intention and confidence.

During this journey, it is common to encounter uncomfortable thoughts and emotions, stories from the past, and anxieties about the future. Navigating these experiences is transformative, contributing to personal growth and resilience. I use various techniques to help manage these moments, such as polyvagal exercises, focused breathing, guided imagery, binaural beats and mindful body movement. You have the flexibility to experiment and discover what works best for you. For example, you might find breathwork most effective before meditation, or starting with journaling may feel more natural. Research consistently supports mindfulness techniques like journaling and meditation in improving focus and productivity.[4] Integrating these practices into daily life allows you to recharge and realign with your goals, cultivating a resilient and productive mindset.

Equally important is creating a suitable workspace at home. This involves setting up a dedicated work area free from distractions and equipped with necessary supportive tools and technology. This dedicated space helps establish boundaries between work and personal life, minimises interruptions and distractions and allows for better focus, motivation and work-flow. Maintaining a clean and organised workspace helps you work more efficiently while working in a cluttered environment can elevate stress levels and reduce focus. When surrounded by mess or loud external noise, our bodies often absorb this stress, impacting us both consciously and subconsciously. Therefore, approach your workspace with creativity and playfulness.

Design a space that reflects your personality and preferences, ensuring it is a place where you feel comfortable, engaged and energised. Feel free to express yourself with decor or items that inspire you. Nowadays, many corporate environments priori-tise ergonomics when designing their workspaces. It is import-ant to also think about this when working from home, ensur-ing that you maintain proper posture and reduce the risk of discomfort or injury even when working remotely. When your workspace lacks proper ergonomic setup, you may sit in awk-ward positions for extended periods, putting strain on your muscles and joints. This can result in discomfort, stiffness and even chronic pain over time. Incorrect posture and repetitive movements can exacerbate these issues, leading to further dis-comfort and potential long-term health problems.

It is intriguing to see an increasing number of young profession-als in their 20s spending long hours at their desks, often suf-fering from chronic neck and back pain. In my practice, I have noticed that these individuals face similar issues. Poor posture and biomechanical imbalances strain the spine's muscles, liga-ments and joints. For instance, prolonged sitting with forward head posture can lead to tightness and fatigue in the neck and upper back, while slouching disrupts the spine's natural curvature, causing muscle imbalances and tension. Over time, these stresses can result in inflammation, chronic pain conditions and migraines. Therefore, addressing ergonomic factors, becoming aware of your posture and including corrective exercises to strengthen and stabilise the spine are essential. Without intervention, young professionals may endure daily pain and risk worsening their conditions as they age, highlighting the need for early action to support musculoskeletal health.

Take a moment to assess your current priorities and ask yourself: Are they aligned with supporting your health? If not, now is the time to make changes that prioritise your well-being and create a foundation for long-term vitality.

As we conclude this chapter, we have explored the essential transition process to remote work. This shift from a traditional office to a remote workspace requires careful consideration of your environment, mindset and tools. In essence, navigating the challenges of remote work requires a blend of intention, flexibility and self-awareness. By thoughtfully establishing your workspace, developing a productive mindset and leveraging the right technologies, you can thrive in this new landscape, all while maintaining a healthy balance between your professional and personal life. Embrace the opportunities this transition brings, and remember that you can shape your remote work experience into a fulfilling and rewarding one.

Now, I invite you to reflect on your current habits and routines. Ask yourself: *Do my actions support the life I aspire to create? What can I do now to make a positive change?*

Remember, every small change you make can significantly improve your working experience. By welcoming this transition with intention and commitment, you will set the stage for a fulfilling and balanced professional and personal life.

Key Points

- **Adaptation beyond circumstance.** Remote work, whether a choice or a necessity, requires intentional adaptation. This shift is not just about location but also about aligning work with personal values.

- **Embracing growth through change.** Moving from a traditional office to remote work involves resilience. It is a process of trial and error where each challenge develops a stronger, more aligned routine and sense of purpose.

- **Balancing relationships and self-care.** Remote work requires active effort to sustain both personal and professional connections. Supportive relationships and self-reflection are essential to maintain balance and well-being in this new work dynamic.

- **Creating work-life balance.** Remote work offers flexibility but requires discipline. Finding a rhythm between freedom and structure helps prevent burnout and supports a fulfilling work-life balance.

- **Building self-discipline and resilience.** Remote work demands self-discipline and intentional time management. Short-term sacrifices often lead to long-term stability and freedom to reach your goals.

- **Prioritising self-care for productivity.** A balanced routine is key to productivity and well-being. Tuning into your body's needs and integrating regular self-care ensures sustained energy and presence in all areas of life.

Chapter 2
Optimising Your Remote Work Environment

"Take care of your body. It's the only place you have to live."
– Jim Rohn

Building on our earlier discussion of ergonomics, this chapter dives deeper into how our bodies react to stress and repetitive movements. It is fascinating how the body, when subjected to prolonged sitting or poorly set up workstations, can adapt in ways we might not notice until discomfort sets in. Whether it is nagging back pain, stiffness in the neck or more serious issues like pinched nerves, these symptoms are often signs that our bodies are struggling with something deeper. This chapter aims to help you understand the physiological complexities behind these reactions and give you practical, proactive steps to prevent musculoskeletal problems before they take hold. It is not just about addressing discomfort at the moment; it is about creating a workspace that supports your body and helps you feel your best day in and day out. This chapter will provide you with a clear roadmap to design an ergonomic and personalised workspace that alleviates physical challenges you may be facing and sets you on the path to improved well-being.

> Ergonomics is the science of designing workplaces, products and systems to fit people's needs, aiming to improve safety, comfort and productivity. It focuses on optimum well-being and system performance by considering posture, physical strain and the overall user experience.

When clients come to me with issues like a pinched nerve, chronic headaches or general discomfort, my first question is always, "Why did this happen?" We start to peel back the layers: Was it the way they have been sitting? Have they been getting quality sleep, and could their mattress or pillow be a factor? There might also be underlying neurological factors contributing to their discomfort, such as hormonal imbalances or deficiencies of essential vitamins and minerals.

Stress often plays a massive role in the body's response to discomfort, as chronic stress can lead to muscle tension, inflammation and weakened immunity, making it harder for the body to recover and adapt. Often, we find that poor ergonomics, lack of movement, lack of quality sleep or high-stress levels are behind these physical symptoms. Our bodies are incredibly resilient and can adapt to stress for quite some time, but eventually, it catches up with us. These issues don't appear out of thin air; they are often the result of accumulated strain and neglected habits. Over time, even slight imbalances can develop into persistent discomfort or chronic issues that demand our attention. That is why, in our sessions, it is never just about treating the immediate pain. We dig deeper, working together to break down the root causes to figure out actionable, manageable steps towards a solution. Whether it is adjusting their workspace setup, working on sleep routines, changing some furniture or managing stress more effectively, it is all part of a larger, more meaningful process. By addressing the real causes behind the discomfort, we don't just aim for temporary relief – we aim for long-term, sustainable health improvements.

When you work or study, do you sit on the floor or struggle to maintain a comfortable position? While many cultures throughout history have embraced sitting on the floor for dining, meditation or social gatherings (such as the traditional *seiza* position in Japan, which symbolises respect, or the cross-legged seating in India that is believed to aid digestion), these practices can sometimes lead to discomfort in the context of modern life. You might also manage with less sleep and rely on coffee to get through the day, thinking your body can handle it. However, as time passes, you may notice your body starting to signal what works and what doesn't. Our bodies naturally change over time, influenced by age, lifestyle and environment, and adapting to these shifts is essential for maintaining well-being.

If you have recently begun working from home and using your laptop extensively, you may have experienced discomfort in your neck and upper back. Repetitive typing, combined with less use of a pen, can lead to strain on your fingers, while prolonged screen time might cause eye discomfort. Since you began working at your desk, you may have noticed changes in your posture, such as slouching or hunching, and you might be unsure how to correct them. Difficulty concentrating due to discomfort or pain can lead to headaches or eye strain by the end of the day, affecting your mood and sleep. Looking back, can you recognise how many days you have taken off due to these challenges? In the long run, these issues can result in fatigue and tiredness, impacting your physical, mental and overall health. The good news is that you don't need to spend a fortune; you simply need to understand the principles of ergonomics and stay attuned to your body's needs.

After all, creating a workspace that prioritises ergonomics is important for long-term comfort and sustained productivity. Recent studies have shown that ergonomic interventions significantly improved clinical outcomes in a worker population affected by lower back problems.[1] Whether you are working in the office or remotely, improper body posture may lead to a significant body malfunction. Remember the principle "form follows function"? It explains that the structure of the human body should directly correspond to its intended function or purpose. If the body's physical structure is compromised (e.g., posture, range of motion (ROM), mobility and flexibility), then the body's natural function becomes impaired and issues may occur. These malfunctions manifest as physical pains, soreness, spasms, cramps, stiffness, tenderness, migraines and other drawbacks.

Consider investing in ergonomic furniture such as adjustable desks and chairs to address these issues. Some items may be pricey, so please do not get discouraged. There are other affordable products, and you can work with what you already have at home. Instead of purchasing a laptop stand, for example, you can place several books underneath it. Initially, I used a stack of books I liked, choosing those with titles and colours that inspired me and brought positivity. From my understanding, many companies compensate employees for their ergonomic setup when working from home, so it is worth checking what support is available, how to access it and when you can expect it.

The truth is, we aren't designed to sit for 8+ hours a day or work 12-hour shifts – it is simply not natural. Our bodies thrive on movement and variety, and prolonged periods of sitting or working without breaks can take a toll on our health. While modern work demands often push us into these patterns, it is important to consciously integrate movement and rest into your routines to maintain your well-being. Understanding your body's needs can create a healthier, more synergetic approach to work and life. I encourage you to take a moment to reflect on your work habits and consider how they impact your body's movement and health.

Incorporating regular breaks throughout your day, along with simple exercises like stretching, can significantly relieve muscle tension and improve your health. Taking the time to step away from your desk, even for just a few minutes, allows your body to reset, preventing the build-up of stiffness or discomfort that often comes with sitting for long periods. Research shows that workplace exercise programmes effectively reduce lower back pain, increase muscle strength and flexibility and improve the quality of life for office workers.[2] To keep it straightforward, set an alarm every hour to remind yourself to get up and stretch or take a short walk – this practice is beneficial whether you are in the office or working from home. Additionally, how we sit impacts our breathing and the function of our diaphragm. Taking regular breaks is also an excellent opportunity to focus on your breathing. When we pause and take deeper breaths, it allows for better oxygen intake and gives our diaphragm room to expand, which is directly linked to our nervous system and the vagus nerve. Proper breathing can affect your mood, helping you feel calmer and more grounded. It also sharpens your focus and concentration, giving you that mental reset to approach tasks with a fresh mindset. So, next time you take a break, take a few deep breaths – you might be surprised at how much it improves your clarity and focus.

Designing an Ergonomic Workspace

As many of us transition to remote work or hybrid arrangements, the importance of designing an environment that supports our physical well-being and enhances our focus has never been clearer. Whether you have a designated home office or work from various spots in your home, understanding how to optimise your workspace can significantly impact your performance and overall health. The information below will guide you through the essential elements of an ergonomic setup, ensuring you can work efficiently and comfortably.

Choose the Right Furniture

Investing in supportive furniture is key to maintaining good posture during long work hours. A chair with adjustable features like lumbar support, armrests and seat height helps distribute body weight evenly and reduces spinal pressure. The size of the chair is also important; it should be appropriately tailored to your body's dimensions and proportions for optimal support and comfort. If you use a regular chair, consider adding a lumbar support cushion, which can make a big difference. I also use one in my car, which has greatly improved my back support. Ergonomic furniture and orthopaedic aids can be affordable and easily integrated into your workspace. Similarly, choosing a desk that allows for proper posture is important. A desk with sufficient surface area ensures you can keep your work essentials within reach without straining or reaching excessively. The desk's height should be adjusted so that your elbows are bent at a 90-degree angle when typing, with your wrists in a neutral position. This angle helps prevent wrist strain and carpal tunnel syndrome.

When furniture is not supportive or properly adjusted, it can lead to a range of musculoskeletal issues. Sitting in a chair without adequate lumbar support can cause slouching, increasing pressure on the spine and leading to discomfort in the lower back.[3] A lack of armrest support may cause shoulder and neck tension, contributing to muscle fatigue and pain.[4] Additionally, a desk that is too high or too low can lead to awkward postures, straining the neck, shoulders and arms. Recent studies have highlighted the importance of ergonomic furniture in preventing such issues. For example, research published in the *Journal of Occupational and Environmental Medicine* found that mismatches between desk and chair proportions, or working with a small computer screen, can worsen musculoskeletal problems and negatively affect performance when working from home.[5] Having these conversations with my clients and helping them adjust their setups has led to noticeable improvements over time, including reduced muscle tension, decreased pain and less stiffness. Correctly positioning the body takes awareness, effort and patience and the positive results are well worth it when guided by the right information.

I recall a client who suffered from a pinched nerve in her neck. This issue not only caused her significant pain and irritation but also interfered with her daily job. She had difficulty sitting at her desk, typing, and even moving, which led to a noticeable decline in her work productivity and increased stress. Upon examining her neck muscles, it was clear that one side was overactive, likely due to sleeping on her stomach – a habit that can lead to spasms in the mid to lower back and worsen nerve problems. She began training herself to sleep on her back and soon noticed significant improvements. Creating new habits involves commitment and a willingness to let go of practices that no longer serve you. By making these conscious changes, my client was able to better her overall well-being and regain comfort in her daily life, leading to better productivity at work.

To adjust a chair properly:

- Ensure your feet are flat on the floor or a footrest and that your knees are bent at a 90-degree angle.

- Adjust the seat height so your hips are slightly higher than your knees.

- Position the lumbar support to fit the natural curve of your lower back.

- Adjust the armrests so that your elbows are bent at a 90-degree angle when resting your arms.

To adjust a desk properly:

- Set the desk at a height that allows your elbows to be bent at a 90-degree angle when typing, with your wrists in a neutral position.

- Ensure the desk surface is clutter-free so your keyboard, mouse and other essentials can be properly placed.

HEIGHT-ADJUSTABLE TABLE POSTURE

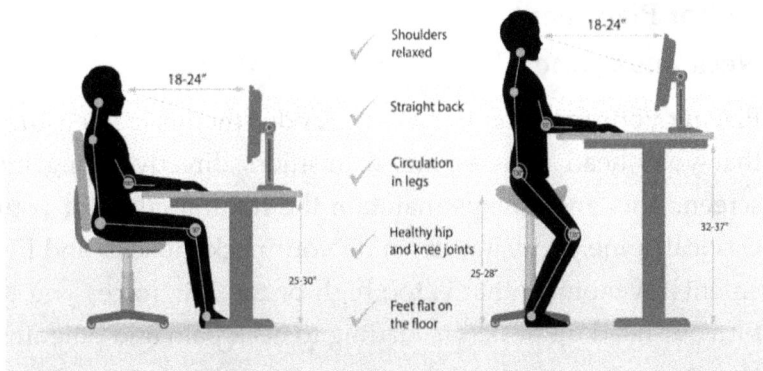

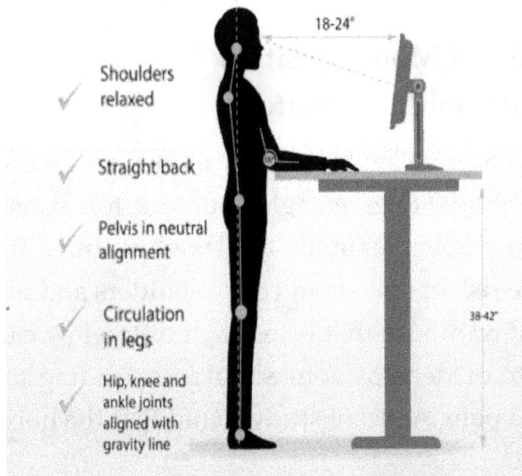

Position Your Equipment Correctly

Keeping the monitor at an appropriate distance (about an arm's length away) helps prevent eye strain and reduces the risk of developing symptoms of Computer Vision Syndrome (CVS), such as dry eyes and headaches. A monitor placed too close or far can cause eye fatigue, headaches and blurred vision due to constant refocusing. Research has shown that a monitor positioned closer than 40 cm to the eyes is positively associated with increased neck pain intensity.[6]

Monitor Placement
Neck and Spine Alignment

Placing your monitor at eye level under the horizon ensures that your head is in a neutral position, directly facing the screen. This angle helps maintain the natural curve of your cervical spine, reducing strain on your neck muscles and ligaments. A monitor that is too high or too low forces you to tilt your head up or down, leading to neck pain and potential long-term musculoskeletal issues.

Keyboard and Mouse Position
Arm and Shoulder Comfort

Positioning your keyboard and mouse so that your elbows are bent at a 90-degree angle and your forearms are parallel to the floor helps maintain a relaxed posture. This setup reduces the risk of tension in your shoulders and upper back. A keyboard or mouse that is too high or too low can cause you to elevate or depress your shoulders, leading to muscle fatigue and pain. A recent study found that the horizontal positioning of the keyboard can influence upper extremity movements, with proper wrist and elbow alignment being better maintained when the keyboard is placed about 8 cm from the edge of the desk.[7]

Wrist Health

Keeping your wrists in a neutral position (not bent up or down) minimises strain on the tendons and nerves in your wrists. Incorrect positioning can result in extended or flexed wrists, increasing the likelihood of repetitive strain injuries (RSIs) such as carpal tunnel syndrome, which can cause pain, numbness and tingling in the hands and fingers.

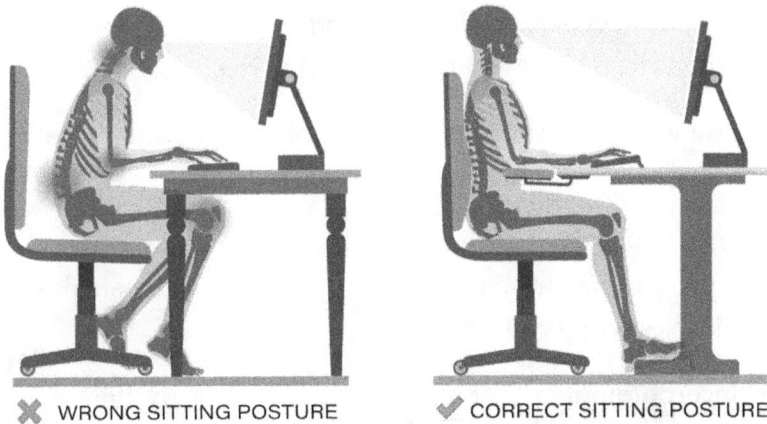

✖ WRONG SITTING POSTURE   ✔ CORRECT SITTING POSTURE

When equipment isn't positioned correctly, your body is forced into awkward postures, leading to cumulative stress on muscles, joints and tendons. This can result in chronic pain, reduced work efficiency and an increased risk of long-term musculoskeletal disorders. Fortunately, work-related musculoskeletal issues can be prevented. By following ergonomic principles and correctly positioning your equipment, you can support your body's natural biomechanics, reduce the risk of injury and create a more comfortable and productive work environment.

Additional tips:

- Use an anti-glare screen or adjust your monitor's brightness and contrast to reduce eye strain caused by glare.

- Position your desk to make the most of natural light while avoiding glare on your screen.

- Consider ergonomic accessories such as an ergonomic mouse, keyboard, or laptop stand to improve comfort and reduce the risk of repetitive strain injuries.

- Use what you already have at home. For example, elevate your laptop by placing it on a stack of books.

- Using a Swiss ball instead of a chair can improve core strength, posture and balance by engaging the stabilising muscles while you sit.

- Incorporate regular breaks into your work routine to rest your eyes, stretch your muscles and change your posture. The 20-20-20 rule is a good practice: every 20 minutes, take a 20-second break to look at something 20 feet away.

- Set an alarm to remind you to stand up, stretch and take a short walk every hour.

- Keep a water bottle and healthy snacks nearby to stay hydrated and fuel your body throughout the day. Proper nutrition and hydration help prevent fatigue and maintain focus.

- You can open a window for fresh air, step into the garden, or take a short stroll down the street.

- Spend a few minutes practising deep belly breathing, which helps stretch the diaphragm and increase oxygen supply.

I encourage you to assess your working environment.

What adjustments can you make right now? What other changes should you consider? Think about your goals and areas for improvement.

Ask yourself: How is my current setup supporting my health?

Make a list and prioritise:

- Changes I can make immediately

- Changes that require purchasing

- What can I realistically afford at the moment, and for which items

---

Separate Your Work Area From Personal Spaces

Creating clear boundaries between your work area and personal spaces is essential for maintaining balance, productivity and a sense of calm. Designating a specific area in your home solely for work – a separate room, a corner, or just a dedicated desk – helps your brain distinguish between work and relaxation. These physical boundaries and visual cues signal your nervous system to shift into "work mode" when you are in that space. This is particularly important for your vagal nerve, which regulates stress and relaxation. A workspace that promotes focus and calm supports your productivity and creates a sense of safety and well-being that helps regulate your autonomic nervous system. When you feel stressed due to work demands, your environment should help to soothe and ground you, creating a space where your nervous system can relax and recover. Surrounding yourself with items that bring comfort or inspiration can make a significant difference, helping you feel safe and at ease while you work.

For example, my workspace is set up near a large window that brings in natural light, which helps me feel energised. I have a board for important notes, personal items that inspire focus and a small corner for meditation to reset when needed. Musical instruments like drums, an African shaker with shells that connect me to the sea and a Tibetan singing bowl are always within reach. Depending on what calls to me at the moment, I will connect with these sounds to ground myself. This setup looks pleasant and soothing and encourages creativity, self-expression and body movement. I have noticed improved concentration, stress levels and overall well-being by aligning my workspace with my needs. So, think about how you might optimise your workspace – not just for productivity but also to encourage relaxation, creativity and resilience. Whether through sound, light or layout, a well-designed space can help support a better vagal tone and a healthier mindset.

Also, make it a habit to take regular breaks during your workday to step away from your desk and do something unrelated to work. It is important to prevent burnout and allow yourself to recharge before diving back into tasks. Think about simple activities like cooking a meal, walking, doing some stretches or a quick workout, listening to music or even taking a short nap or shower to refresh your mind and body. For example, in Japan, taking a nap during work hours is considered acceptable, while in Spain, the afternoon rest or *siesta* is a cherished cultural practice. Just because these habits aren't part of the culture we grew up with doesn't mean we can't embrace different perspectives and make them work for us. Also, including mindfulness practices, like meditation or deep breathing, can help you shift gears between work and personal time. These small moments of mindfulness can make it easier to disconnect from work and fully enjoy your personal life when you are off the clock.

Another way to separate your working area from your personal space is to create boundaries around your work schedule by setting specific start and end times for your workday and sticking to them as much as possible. When working from home, communicate them to your household members, as this helps prevent interruptions during designated work times and al-

lows for focused productivity. Also, communicate your boundaries with co-workers, clients, or supervisors to establish expectations around availability and response times. Let them know
when you will be accessible for work-related tasks and when
you will be offline for personal time. I always put my phone
on silent mode when I need privacy while working. This way, I
avoid the temptation to constantly check emails, text messages,
Amazon deals and other notifications.

I must confess to a funny habit: I have always been an early
riser, usually around 5:30 am, sometimes even earlier if Pump-
kin, the cat, needs to go out. I am ready to rock'n'roll, assuming
the rest of the world is too. I often find myself replying to messages sent by friends or clients the night before, ticking these
tasks off for the day so early that my friends have joked about it
for a long time. Since creating my boundaries, I now use those
peaceful morning hours for self-care and preparing mindfully
for the day ahead.

Another good tip is to create rituals or routines to mark the beginning and end of your workday. This could include a morning coffee ritual to start the day or a brief walk around the block
to signify the end of the workday and transition into your personal time. A warm lemon water in the morning, usually 5:30
am, is my way of starting the day. Although I prefer juicing and
blending, the noise would wake the dead early in the morning!
So, I typically begin juicing around 7 am. By then, I had already
had a shower, gotten myself dressed and ready to hit the gym,
and completed my morning routine. Once I have had my gin-
ger shot and juice, I feel fully prepared to face the world. This
routine remains consistent even during the winter, although

I might adjust by changing my nutrition plan to support my well-being and physical performance in the colder weather, as I enjoy feeling warm and energised.

Then, at the end of the day, I finish my body treatment routine, reflect on the day and journal. This is my self-care moment – a time to look after myself and, in a way, reward myself with love and care. Everyone has unique preferences, desires and requirements, whether going to the gym, attending a group class, playing sports, practising mindfulness or socialising with friends and family. Finding what truly resonates with you and supports your well-being is essential; discover the practices that energise and ground you, and let those become the foundation of your routine.

After considering these points, take a moment to reflect on what works best for you. Envision your ideal workday and how it supports your productivity, creativity, health and overall well-being. Consider your preferred work environment, daily routine, breaks and self-care practices. Understanding your needs and aspirations allows you to tailor your workday to optimise your professional success and personal fulfilment.

Incorporating Inspiration and Creativity Into Your Workspace

In today's fast-paced world, the design of your workspace can make a difference in boosting your creativity and keeping you inspired. A workspace that helps you get things done and sparks innovative thinking is key to personal and professional growth. Personally, I love the process of setting up a work-space that encourages creative expression. The best part is that it doesn't have to cost a fortune. With a bit of imagination and a clear sense of what works best for you, you can create a space that truly supports and energises your work.

Here are some strategies to incorporate elements of inspiration and creativity into your workspace design:

Embrace Natural Light and Fresh Air

Natural light profoundly impacts our mood, energy levels and overall sense of well-being. Studies have shown that exposure to natural light can improve creativity and productivity by reducing fatigue and increasing alertness.[8] Position your desk near a window, if possible, to maximise the natural light you receive throughout the day. Additionally, ensure proper ventilation to allow fresh air to circulate in your workspace, which can help keep your mind clear and focused.

Personalise Your Space

Your workspace should reflect your personality and interests, making it a place where you feel comfortable and inspired. Incorporate personal items such as photographs, artwork, or memorabilia that bring you joy and remind you of your passions and achievements. Include favourite quotes or books or create a vision board.

These items can serve as visual reminders of your goals and the reasons behind your hard work, boosting your motivation and creativity. Consider how you can further personalise your space to reflect your unique personality and passions.

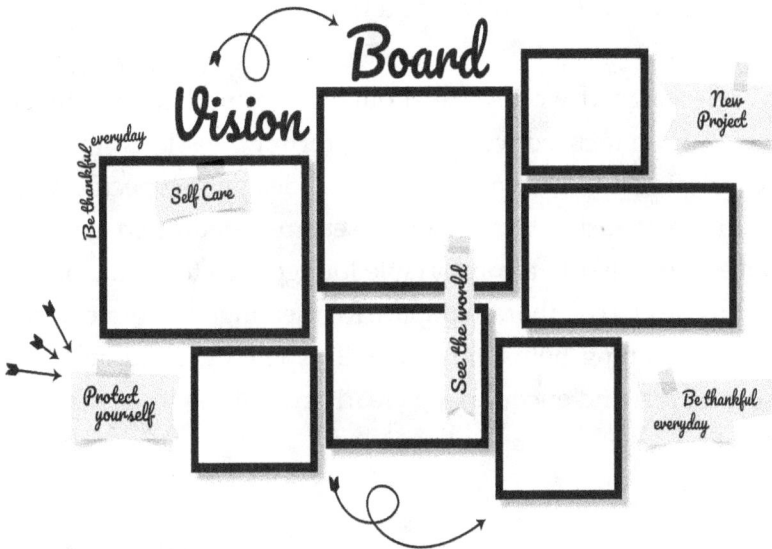

Integrate Plants and Greenery

Incorporating plants into your workspace enhances visual appeal and offers several psychological benefits. Plants can reduce stress, improve air quality and boost feelings of happiness and tranquillity. You can opt for low-maintenance varieties such as succulents, snake plants, or pothos, which thrive indoors and require minimal care.

Greenery can create a calming environment, helping you think more clearly and creatively. Looking after living things, even in the form of a plant, requires care, love and compassion. You need to open your heart and nurture this life, much like how we tend to our growth. It is a simple yet profound way to stay connected with the cycle of growth and renewal.

Create Zones for Different Activities

A well-designed workspace should accommodate various activities, from focused work to brainstorming sessions. To create a dynamic and flexible environment, designate specific areas for different tasks. For example, set up a dedicated desk for concentrated work, a comfortable lounge area for relaxation or reading, and a collaborative space for meetings and brainstorming. This zoning helps you mentally switch gears, improving productivity and encouraging creativity.

Use Colour Strategically

Colour psychology significantly influences our emotions and creativity. Different colours can evoke various responses; for example, blue and green promote calmness and focus, while yellow and orange stimulate creativity and energy. Choose a colour palette that resonates with you and supports the type of work you do. Whether through wall paint, furniture, or decorative accents, incorporating the right colours can create an environment that inspires and energises you.

Incorporate Inspirational Quotes and Art

Surrounding yourself with motivational quotes and artwork can be a constant source of inspiration. Choose quotes that align with your values and aspirations and display them prominently in your workspace. Similarly, select artwork that you find uplifting and thought-provoking. These visual elements can offer mental boosts throughout the day, nurturing a positive mindset and encouraging a creative approach to problem-solving. Perhaps there are some elements from nature that you can incorporate to lift your space as well.

Incorporate Technology Thoughtfully

While technology is essential for modern work, it can also become a distraction if not managed well. Organise your tech tools to support productivity without cluttering your space. Use cable management solutions to keep cords tidy and invest in quality hardware that improves your work experience. Consider incorporating smart devices that can automate tasks and streamline your workflow, allowing you to focus more on creative endeavours. Ask yourself how to cultivate community and collaboration within your workspace, whether you work solo or with a team.

Regularly Refresh Your Space

Even the most inspiring workspace can become stale over time. Regularly updating and refreshing your environment can keep it feeling new and invigorating. Rearrange your furniture, introduce new decor items, or simply declutter to maintain a clean and organised space. These small changes can significantly impact your mental state and improve your creative output. Changing your work environment after finishing bigger projects symbolises a fresh beginning. It invites a new wave of energy, creating the space for fresh ideas and momentum as you transition into your next endeavours.

By reflecting on your unique needs and aspirations and implementing these strategies, you can create a workspace that ignites creativity, supports well-being and elevates your work to new heights. Remember, your workspace is more than just a physical area – it reflects your ambitions, a driver of your success and a foundation for sustaining balance and productivity. Prioritising ergonomics helps prevent discomfort and long-term strain, ensuring your body is supported throughout each workday.

Establishing clear boundaries between work and personal spaces encourages mental clarity and helps maintain a healthy work-life balance, signalling to your mind when it is time to focus and when to unwind. Equally important is incorporating regular breaks to recharge, stretch and recalibrate, which boosts focus, reduces fatigue and helps you stay energised over the long term.

You set yourself up for productivity and a fulfilling and balanced professional journey by thoughtfully crafting a workspace that inspires and sustains you.

Key Points

- **Prioritise ergonomics for comfort and health.** Ergonomics goes beyond comfort; it supports your physical well-being. Proper posture, supportive furniture and well-positioned equipment reduce strain and prevent long-term issues. By following ergonomic principles, you create a sustainable workspace that promotes comfort and productivity.

- **Set clear work-life boundaries.** Designating a dedicated workspace signals when to focus and when to relax, helping you maintain a balanced routine. These boundaries create mental clarity and ease, supporting your productivity and well-being.

- **Embrace regular breaks for energy and focus.** Frequent breaks reduce tension and boost focus. Even a brief stretch or deep breath resets your mind and body, preventing fatigue and improving productivity, allowing you to approach tasks with fresh energy.

- **Personalise your workspace for inspiration.** Creating a workspace that reflects your personality inspires motivation and creativity. Meaningful touches, like quotes, plants, or artwork, boost mood and remind you of your goals, turning your workspace into a source of energy and inspiration.

- **Integrate nature and natural light.** Natural light and fresh air lift your mood and creativity. Position your desk by a window to reduce fatigue and increase alertness. Plants or natural elements also create a calming, balanced environment that nurtures well-being.

- **Cultivate intentional routines and reflection.** Establishing a consistent routine supports focus and growth. Regular self-reflection helps you adapt, ensuring your routines and environment align with your evolving goals while supporting your productivity and resilience.

Chapter 3
Nervous System and Mindfulness: Balancing Work and Well-being

"Between stimulus and response there is a space. In that space is our power to choose our response. In our response lies our growth and our freedom".
– Viktor Frankl

Let us start with our bodies because this is where everything truly begins. Our bodies are our first and most constant point of interaction with ourselves and the world around us. The more we tune into our bodies, the more we understand the deep connection between our physical sensations, thoughts, and emotions. At the core of this connection lies our primal brain, influenced heavily by the sympathetic nervous system, which governs our survival instincts. This part of our brain is always on high alert, constantly scanning for danger, threats, or signs of safety, often triggering habitual and automatic responses without our conscious awareness. These ingrained reactions help us navigate the world quickly but can also keep us stuck in cycles of stress, fear, and reactivity. They shape how we think, feel, and behave, dictating our reactions to people, events and circumstances, whether rushing through office tasks or juggling remote work demands. By understanding this connection, we can manage our responses more mindfully, moving through work and life with greater awareness and stability. Tuning into our bodies allows us to recognise when our survival instincts are in overdrive and consciously shift towards a more relaxed, focused state.

Stress plays a crucial role in the health and well-being of working professionals, particularly those in high-demand environments or remote settings. While some stress can motivate, chronic stress can wear down mental and physical health, affecting productivity, focus, and resilience. For those working remotely, stress can stem from isolation, blurred work-life boundaries, and the pressure to remain constantly available. This prolonged stress response activates the body's survival mechanisms, releasing hormones like adrenaline and cortisol to prepare for action. These hormones increase heart rate, blood pressure and energy availability by drawing on glucose reserves. However, when this state of heightened alert persists, it can lead to issues such as hypertension, sleep disruptions, digestive problems and even burnout. Understanding this physiological cascade helps professionals realise the impact of stress on their bodies and underscores the importance of incorporating stress management techniques, such as mindfulness and regular breaks, to maintain long-term health and productivity.

This diagram highlights the path of the vagus nerve, which connects the brain to various key organs throughout the body. It branches out to influence areas such as the heart, lungs,

STRESS RESPONSE

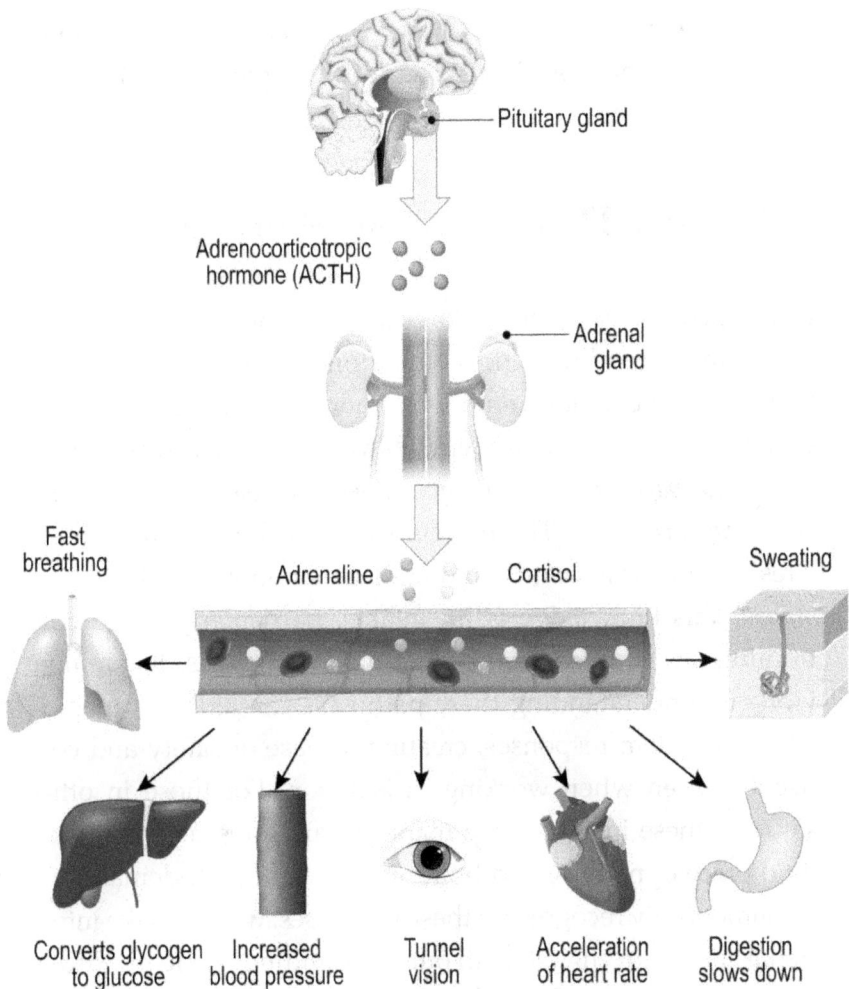

Pituitary gland

Adrenocorticotropic hormone (ACTH)

Adrenal gland

Fast breathing

Adrenaline

Cortisol

Sweating

Converts glycogen to glucose

Increased blood pressure

Tunnel vision

Acceleration of heart rate

Digestion slows down

stomach, liver, and intestines, playing a crucial role in regulating essential functions like digestion, heart rate, and respiratory rate. The vagus nerve is central to the body's parasympathetic "rest and digest" response, promoting relaxation and recovery.

This pathway is integral to polyvagal theory, which explores how these connections impact our physiological and emotional responses to stress.

Polyvagal Theory at Your Workspace

Developed by Dr Stephen Porges, this theory provides a profound understanding of how our autonomic nervous system influences our behaviour, emotions, and social interactions. Porges identifies three primary circuits within the nervous system: *the ventral vagal complex, the sympathetic nervous system,* and *the dorsal vagal complex.*[1] These circuits regulate how we respond to stress, form social bonds, and manage emotional and physical states. This knowledge is invaluable, particularly when confronting stress, burnout, or emotional challenges. For remote workers, understanding these pathways can aid in managing nervous system responses, creating a sense of safety and connection, even when working in isolation. For those in office settings, these insights help manage daily pressures, navigate workplace dynamics, and build resilience in high-demand environments. By recognising these responses, we can make intentional choices to engage with our surroundings more mindfully and constructively. This awareness allows us to remain grounded in our bodies while fully present and connected with others. Since the autonomic nervous system operates largely outside our conscious control, we must actively work to recognise and understand how these shifts manifest in us. This means working on self-awareness, regularly checking in with our internal states and practising techniques that support regulation, such as breathwork, mindfulness, and grounding exercises. With commitment and practice, we can develop a deeper understanding of our responses, creating space for healthier, more adaptive ways of interacting with our environment and ourselves.

Hierarchy of Response

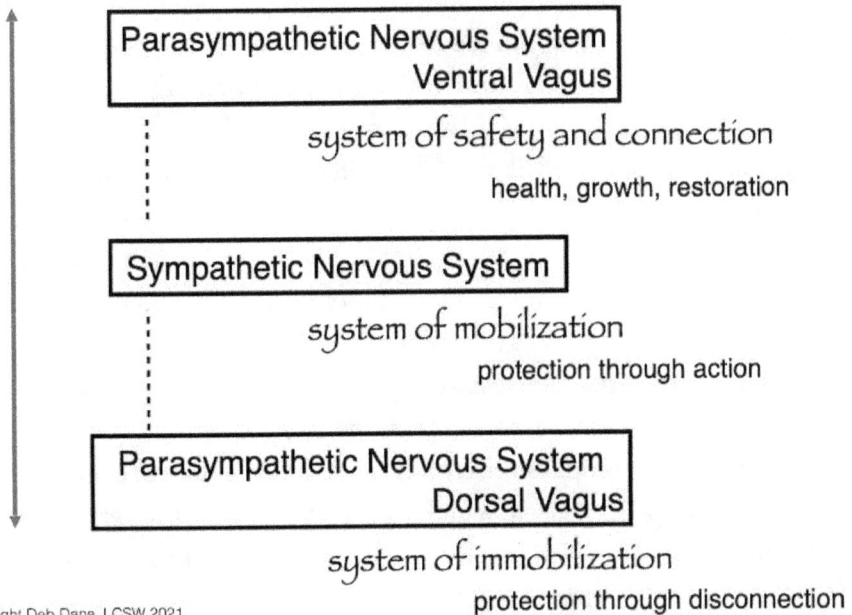

Parasympathetic Nervous System
Ventral Vagus

system of safety and connection

health, growth, restoration

Sympathetic Nervous System

system of mobilization

protection through action

Parasympathetic Nervous System
Dorsal Vagus

system of immobilization

protection through disconnection

This image shows the nervous system's *Hierarchy of Response*. At the top, the Ventral Vagus supports safety, connection, and restoration. The Sympathetic Nervous System in the middle facilitates mobilisation for protection through action. At the base, the Dorsal Vagus triggers immobilisation for protection through disconnection. These states are dynamic, and we naturally shift through them both consciously and unconsciously, influenced by our internal and external environments and past or present traumas.

How Polyvagal Theory Transformed My Approach

The essence of polyvagal theory is simple but profound: It invites us to tune into our bodies and notice our physical sensations without getting lost in the past or worrying about the future. I first encountered this concept while working on my MSc dissertation, and it was truly life-changing. At that time, I was experiencing frequent panic attacks as I navigated university during the pandemic, dealing with lockdowns, social restrictions, and the pressures of academic and professional life. My nervous system was overwhelmed, and it showed up in the form of panic attacks. Despite my resilience, I realised that resilience alone wasn't enough. I needed to approach myself with kindness and compassion. That is when I discovered Deb Dana's Polyvagal exercises, which helped me start a conversation with my nervous system. By listening to what my body was telling me, the panic attacks gradually subsided, and I haven't experienced one since. I later had the opportunity to train with Deb Dana in person in London, where I learned to apply polyvagal theory in practical ways. What I love most about this approach is its accessibility – it is clear, relatable and something everyone can integrate into their lives. It is about connecting with and understanding your body and how you engage with the world. It is about realising that your body is not just a thing but a dynamic process that tells a story. And that story is yours to understand, shape, and nurture. The answers you seek are already within you, waiting for you to listen.

"The body will recognise when it feels safe."
– Stephen Porges

Polyvagal theory revolves around three key principles that offer insight into how our nervous system influences our behaviour and interactions. One of these principles is *co-regulation*, a fundamental aspect of human survival that involves connecting with others to create a shared sense of safety and comfort. Think of it as our nervous system saying, "We are in this together." Guided by *neuroception* – our brain's subconscious scanning of the environment – our nervous system constantly looks for safety or danger cues in our surroundings and interactions. When we co-regulate with others, whether through a comforting presence, a soothing voice or a reassuring touch, we signal to our nervous system that we are safe, helping to calm the primal brain's constant alertness.[2]

This process is intricately linked to the *Autonomic Hierarchy*, which maps how our autonomic nervous system shifts between different states – feeling safe and connected, preparing to fight or flee or shutting down in response to perceived threats. These shifts profoundly impact how we feel and respond, both physically and emotionally.[3] Co-regulation keeps us anchored in the more balanced and connected states of this hierarchy, allowing us to engage with others and handle stress in healthier, more adaptive ways. These shared moments of connection – small, often unspoken exchanges – help us build resilience, manage life's ups and downs and nurture our overall well-being. When we understand the power of co-regulation, we begin to see how essential our connections are – helping us move beyond a survival-driven state and teaching us how to truly thrive in the world. The Autonomic Hierarchy gives us a deeper understanding of how our nervous system drives our behaviours, emotions, and interactions. It is like a map showing how we move through different states based on what is happening around us – and within us.

Hierarchy in Action

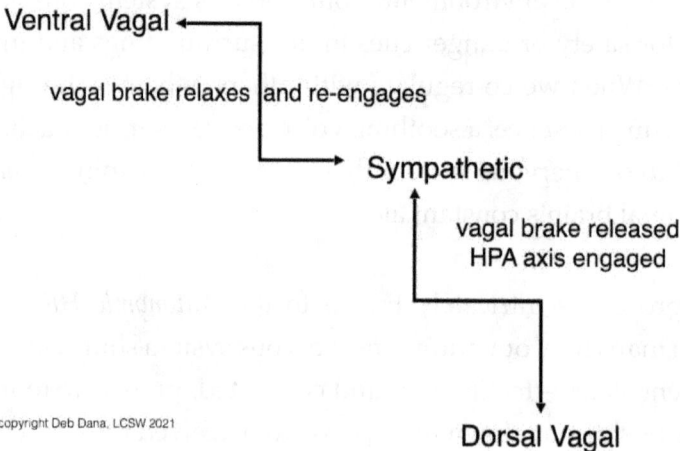

Ventral Vagal

vagal brake relaxes and re-engages

Sympathetic

vagal brake released
HPA axis engaged

Dorsal Vagal

This image illustrates the body's dynamic process of shifting through the states in response to varying levels of safety and threat, demonstrating how it adjusts its reactions to navigate and manage different situations.

1. Ventral Vagal Complex (VVC): This part of the parasympathetic nervous system helps us feel safe, connected and grounded. Often called the "rest and digest" state, it is the calm and engaged place we reach when our body senses safety. Our heart rate slows, digestion improves and we feel more open to connecting with others. We remain fully present in our bodies while genuinely connecting with others.

Imagine those moments when you feel content, inspired, or deeply connected – your body feels light, your breathing steady, and your mind clear. Simple practices like deep, slow breathing can activate the vagus nerve, shifting us into this state and helping us manage stress more easily.[4] Take a moment to recall when you felt this way. What physical cues did your body give you? How did it feel to be truly present? Write down your thoughts – these insights are the stepping stones to understanding your body's signals.

> **Exercise**: Take 8-10 breaths with long inhalations and short exhalations. Notice the subtle signals your nervous system sends. Does it feel more settled, calm, or clear?
>
> This breathing pattern activates VVC.

2. Sympathetic Nervous System (SNS): This system kicks in when we feel threatened or overwhelmed. The fight-or-flight response is designed to keep us safe in danger but also revs up during everyday stress. Rapid breathing, a racing heart, and muscle tension indicate that our sympathetic state is active.

Think about a stressful day at work or when you have felt burnt out. Your body goes into overdrive, leaving you feeling frazzled, on edge, and sometimes even short-tempered. Reflecting on these sensations helps us recognise when we are stuck in this heightened state.

Noticing how your body responds to stress and identifying the associated emotions and thoughts is the first step towards understanding these reactions. By naming and recognising these responses, you can gain insight into your stress patterns and take proactive steps to manage them.

> **Exercise**: Try 8 -10 breaths with short inhalations and longer exhalations. Pay attention to how your body responds – what shifts do you notice? Write down your observations.
>
> This breathing pattern activates SNS.

3. Dorsal Vagal Complex (DVC): This is where the nervous system takes us when we feel overwhelmed or trapped, often without us even realising it. It is the body's way of shutting down to protect itself when fight-or-flight doesn't work.

Ever felt completely drained after a period of high stress, like your body just cannot keep up anymore? That is the DVC stepping in, causing a sense of numbness or disconnection. It is a protective state, but staying here too long can leave us feeling isolated and stuck. I remember times when stress built up so much that I'd go from feeling hyper-alert to completely shutting down, unable to move forward. The more I learned about these shifts, the more I realised how important it is to catch the signs early and give myself permission to rest. This isn't a weakness; it is your body's wisdom asking you to slow down and reconnect.

Exercise: Reflect on how your body feels when moving from a state of high alert to one of exhaustion. What cues does your body give you? How does it feel to shift between these states? Write down your insights and start to recognise these patterns in your daily life.

Stress Curve

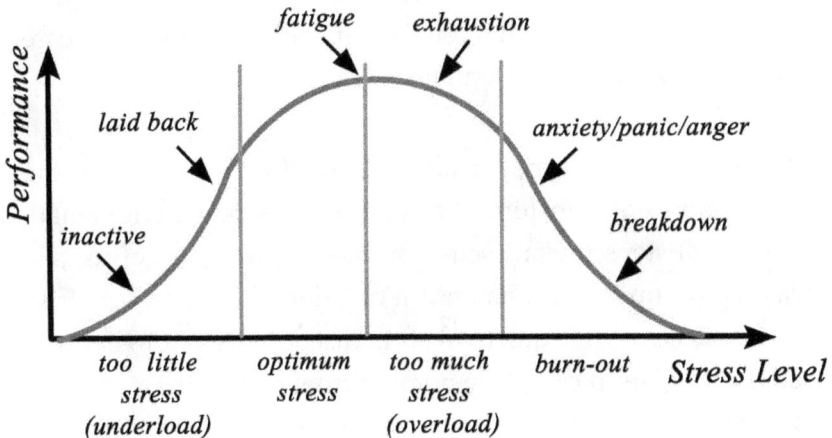

This image depicts the "Stress Curve," which illustrates how performance varies with different stress levels. Moderate stress enhances focus and productivity, while too little or too much stress can lead to low performance or burnout. The curve highlights the importance of balanced stress for optimal functioning.

For those of us working remotely, these principles are especially relevant. Without the daily meaningful human interaction that keeps our ventral vagal complex engaged, it is easy to slip into feelings of disconnection or burnout. I have seen this repeatedly in my professional practice – remote work blurs the lines between personal and professional life, leaving us always "on" and often in a state of low-level stress. Reflecting on my journey, I used to think pushing through was a sign of strength, but I have learned that true strength comes from listening to our bodies and setting boundaries without guilt. It is about taking those moments to pause, breathe and reset – honouring our needs instead of overriding them. If we don't take control of our time and energy, someone else will. So, tune into your nervous system, listen to what it tells you, and remember: self-care isn't indulgence – it is essential.

My client Nuri's journey is also a powerful reminder that the most significant transformations sometimes begin with small, intentional steps toward self-awareness. Like many of us, she was caught up in the momentum of a demanding career, striving for success while quietly feeling disconnected from her true self. Her wake-up call came not just from her unhappiness but also through her body's signals – symptoms of an autoimmune condition that she could no longer ignore. Rather than pushing through or dismissing her health concerns as another inconvenience, Nuri paused, listened and made a radical shift. It was not easy. Leaving the familiar security of her corporate job to study naturopathic nutrition and start over was a leap into the unknown but also a leap towards authenticity. What I admire most about Nuri is her commitment to self-care – not just as a one-time fix but as a daily practice of tuning into her body's needs. She recognised that her condition wasn't just a medical diagnosis; it was a message from her body urging her to slow down, nourish herself, and align her lifestyle with her values.

This isn't something we are often taught. We are conditioned to believe that success looks like constant productivity, but Nuri's journey reminds us that true success is about finding balance and honouring our well-being. It is about understanding that our body's signals are not obstacles to be overcome but messages that guide us towards more meaningful choices. In embracing her new path, Nuri also discovered the power of breathwork – a practice that became a cornerstone of her healing. Breathwork taught her to connect with her body more deeply, helping her navigate not just physical health but the emotional and mental stresses of everyday life. As a breathwork coach, she now helps others do the same, guiding them to find calm amid chaos, reconnect with themselves, and approach challenges with a sense of presence and resilience.

Nuri's story and my own experience with breathwork stand as a testament to the transformative power of aligning with our inner truth and prioritising our well-being. It proves that investing in practices that nurture our health and support our personal growth opens the door to a more fulfilling and balanced life.

Reflecting on her journey, I see a lesson for all of us: It is never too late to make changes that honour your well-being. It is okay to pause, reassess, and choose a different path that prioritises health, happiness, and purpose over the expectations of others. We don't have to wait for a health crisis or burnout to start listening to our bodies. We can begin today, in small ways, by paying attention to how we feel, setting boundaries, and nurturing ourselves with compassion. The journey isn't always straightforward and often involves navigating discomfort and uncertainty. But as Nuri's story shows, when you prioritise your well-being and stay true to yourself, the rewards are profound.

Strategies to Strengthen Ventral Vagal Complex Activation

Breath

Engaging in deep, slow breathing exercises is a powerful way to activate the VVC, creating a state of calm and relaxation. Techniques like diaphragmatic breathing or paced breathing can help ease stress and anxiety by shifting the body from a state of sympathetic arousal (fight or flight) to a more restful parasympathetic state.[5]

Regularly practising these breathing methods helps create a sense of balance and tranquillity, countering the effects of chronic stress and improving overall well-being. I have found that taking just a few minutes each day to focus on my breath can transform how I handle stress, offering a quick reset that makes a big difference in my daily life.

Touch

Physical touch, whether a hug, a massage, or simply placing a hand on your heart, can stimulate the vagus nerve and build up feelings of safety and connection. Touch therapy has been proven to lower cortisol levels, the stress hormone and boost oxytocin, often called the "bonding hormone." This increase in oxytocin supports social bonding and helps reduce stress.[6]

Integrating touch into your daily routine can thus play a vital role in promoting emotional well-being and strengthening a sense of connection. Something as simple as a comforting hug, a gentle hand on your shoulder, or booking a massage as an act of self-care can instantly lift your mood and help you feel more grounded and relaxed.

Movement

Regular physical activity, like yoga, tai chi, or simple stretching, can help regulate the autonomic nervous system. Movement practices incorporating mindfulness and body awareness are particularly effective in activating the VVC. These activities can improve mood, reduce stress, and support overall well-being.[7] Making movement part of your routine can improve your emotional resilience and maintain a steadier state of calm that carries through the rest of your day.

Play

Participating in playful activities and social interactions can significantly stimulate the VVC. Laughter, creative expression, and light-hearted social activities boost emotional regulation, strengthen social bonds and alleviate stress.[8] Incorporating play into your life not only improves your mood but also supports a balanced, resilient state of well-being. Play reminds us that sometimes, the best way to manage stress is to allow ourselves to enjoy life's simple pleasures.

I encourage you to explore these strategies to activate your VVC, manage stress, and establish healthier work habits. Reflect on how these practices can improve your daily routine. If you find starting new habits challenging, consider investing in a personal trainer, a coach, a therapist or joining some other groups. These steps can be valuable for your well-being. Incorporating deep breathing, mindful movement and playful interactions into your life will boost your resilience and contribute to a more supportive remote work environment. Small changes can lead to significant improvements, helping you achieve a more stable and fulfilling work life. From my own experience, I have seen how integrating these practices can transform stress management and improve overall satisfaction. The journey to well-being is personal, but with these strategies, you can find your path to a more grounded and joyful life.

POLYVAGAL EXERCISES

During my training with Deb Dana, she guided me and others through these exercises and taught us how to use them effectively for ourselves and our clients.

Exercise #1: Stop for a moment and notice your neuroception. Take in the environment through sight and sound. See the people and things around you.[9]

What are the cues of safety and danger? Are there enough cues of safety to bring you into a readiness for connection? Or do the cues of danger keep you poised for protection?

Use this question to look through the lens of discernment: in this moment, with this person, in this place, surrounded by these things, are you actually in danger, or are you safe?

Exercise #2: Consider an experience and make your way to the river's source. Bring perception into your neuroception that was the starting point. What was the cue of safety or danger that you followed downstream into feeling, behaviour and finally, story? Give a name to each cue, emotion or thought.[10]

Tip: Journal your experiences and observations. Journaling helps with self-reflection, emotional processing, goal setting, creativity, and memory enhancement. It is a tool for personal growth, supporting self-awareness, and organising your thoughts and ideas.

Making Mindfulness a Daily Habit

Now that we have explored the core principles of polyvagal theory and how our nervous system navigates through various states, let us examine how mindfulness integrates with this framework and why it is important for today's working professionals.

Mindfulness, introduced to psychology by Jon Kabat-Zinn, encourages us to tune into our bodies and emotions, offering a fresh perspective that sees us not as broken but as whole.[11] This practice involves listening to the signals your nervous system sends and responding with kindness and curiosity. By embracing mindfulness, you are befriending your nervous system and learning to understand and accept yourself in all your complexity.

"Mindfulness is the awareness that emerges through paying attention on purpose, in the present moment, and nonjudgmentally to the unfolding of experience moment by moment."
– J. Kabat-Zinn

The reality is that our work environments have changed significantly, particularly with the recent shift to remote work. These changes can be overwhelming, challenging our time management skills, goal-setting abilities, and self-care routines. I have faced similar struggles – setting unrealistic goals or making excuses that only reinforced a cycle of self-doubt and negative self-perception. This cycle can become a self-fulfilling prophecy, shaping how we see ourselves and interact with the world. As Henry Ford wisely said, *"Whether you think you can or you think you can't – you're right."* Our beliefs shape our reality. To break this cycle, nurturing a more realistic and positive self-view is essential.

Mindful awareness plays an important role here. It activates regions of the frontal brain, improving our ability to plan, solve problems, and make informed decisions. For remote workers, this can mean setting clear, manageable goals for the day, managing your time effectively, and making thoughtful decisions about your workload. You can interrupt automatic, habitual responses by becoming more aware of your thoughts and feelings without judgment or reactivity. For instance, if you react to a challenging email with immediate frustration, mindfulness allows you to pause and consider a more measured response. This reduces cognitive distortions and helps you approach difficult conversations, meetings, or tasks with greater compassion and neutrality. Mindfulness enables you to experience uncomfortable feelings, like isolation or stress, without self-criticism and promotes better mental and physical health. This practice is especially beneficial for those working from home, as it encourages regular breaks for mindful activities such as stretching, deep breathing, or brief walks, which can alleviate stress and boost productivity. Mindfulness evolves with you, offering profound benefits both personally and professionally, and helps create a holistic, resilient approach to remote work.

Being attuned to your body means being mindful and compassionate as you observe your nervous system's signals. This awareness helps you recognise when you are shifting between states – whether moving from a calm ventral vagal state to stress or shutdown. Integrating mindfulness into your daily routine can activate the ventral vagal complex (VVC), manage stress more effectively and establish healthier work habits. This improves your well-being and creates a more supportive and productive work environment.

I encourage you to explore these mindfulness strategies and reflect on your habits. Consider moments when you have felt overwhelmed or doubted yourself. Recognise these as signals from your nervous system and approach them with an open, non-judgmental mindset. Understanding where your habits, thoughts, and behaviours originate helps you navigate them with greater awareness and compassion. This practice is not about perfection but about progress and self-discovery.

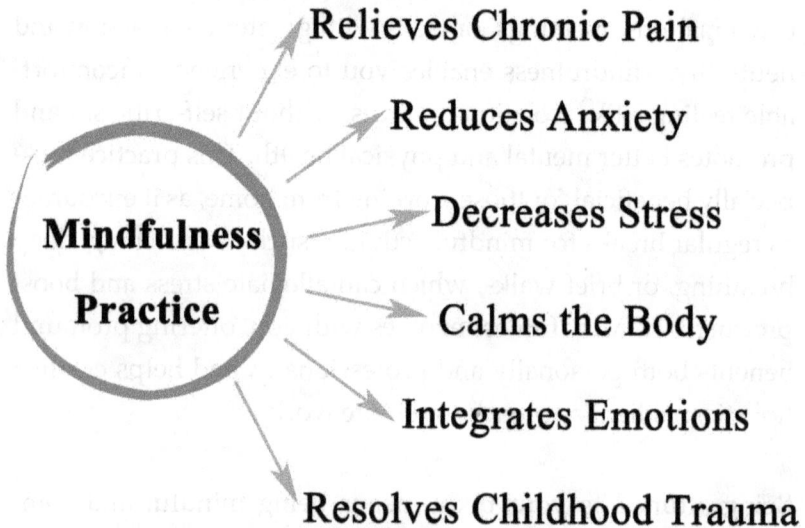

Relieves Chronic Pain

Reduces Anxiety

Mindfulness Practice

Decreases Stress

Calms the Body

Integrates Emotions

Resolves Childhood Trauma

Mindfulness helps you peel back layers of self-doubt and negativity, revealing a deeper understanding of yourself. It is a journey of befriending your nervous system, accepting yourself fully, and recognising that sometimes we need to journey through darker times to see the light. By incorporating mindful practices – whether through deep breathing, physical activity, or simply tuning into your emotions – you start to understand your unique rhythm and needs. This deeper self-awareness empowers you to make changes from a place of genuine understanding rather than judgment.

In essence, embracing these practices helps build a more resilient and steady nervous system better equipped to handle the demands of remote work. It creates a work environment that values well-being and encourages productivity and satisfaction. Reflect on what truly matters to you, set achievable goals, and embrace the process of self-improvement with compassion and patience. Remember, every step you take towards mindfulness is a step towards a more fulfilling and harmonious life. And don't hesitate to reach out for help – whether from a therapist, coach, or holistic practitioner. Seeking support is a valuable investment in yourself and your journey towards well-being.

Reflective Questions

1. **Deep breathing exercises:** How often do you currently practice deep breathing, and how might you integrate it into your daily routine to better manage stress?

2. **Mindful movement:** What types of mindful movement practices resonate with you, and how can you incorporate them into your schedule to support your well-being?

3. **Physical touch:** How can you incorporate more physical touch into your daily life to enhance your sense of connection and well-being?

4. **Playful activities:** What playful activities bring you joy, and how can you make time for these activities to boost your emotional well-being?

5. **Reflective journaling:** How can journaling about your daily experiences and feelings help you better understand your stressors and improve your self-awareness?

6. **Nutrition:** How does your current diet impact your mood and energy levels, and what changes can you make to ensure your nutrition supports your overall well-being?

7. **Sleep:** Are you getting enough quality sleep, and what adjustments can you make to improve your sleep hygiene and ensure you are well-rested?

8. **Reaching out for support:** Who in your network – such as a breath coach, life coach, or other holistic practitioner – can you reach out to for guidance, and how might their support help you achieve a more self-aware approach to your work and life?

This journey is yours – unique, personal, and constantly unfolding. When you set your mind in motion and fuel it with curiosity and discoveries, you tap into your true power and begin to design the life you truly want. Our conditioning and past experiences often create patterns we follow unconsciously, shaping how we think, feel, and act. But by stepping back and observing through mindfulness, you can rewrite your story, guiding your life based on conscious choices rather than old habits or societal expectations.

Remember, your body is not just static; it is an ongoing process – a living, breathing narrative that you can tune into through mindful practices. This is body storytelling: paying attention to your body's signals and using them as a guide for moving forward. If you don't take charge of your time, someone else will decide how it's spent. If you don't stand firm in your values, others will impose theirs on you. It is about letting go of what you think you should do and instead tuning into what truly feels right for you – following your own purpose and mission rather than external pressures.

So, how do you nurture your brain and body? Are you setting the standards that reflect your deepest needs and desires? What boundaries do you establish to protect your energy and well-being? The answers lie in how well you listen to yourself and how willing you are to act in alignment with what you discover. This isn't about perfection; it is about progress, and it is okay to take small steps. Every mindful choice you make helps you craft a life that feels true to who you are. Embrace this journey with patience and compassion, knowing each day offers a new opportunity to grow, create, and connect with your authentic self. Bring that vision to life!

Key Points

- **The power of awareness in the body.** Listening to your body is the first step to navigating life's complexities with wisdom and ease. Tuning into physical sensations helps you recognise stress, understand emotions, and find balance.

- **Understanding the impact of chronic stress on well-being.** Chronic stress wears down mental and physical health, diminishing focus, productivity, and resilience. Recognise when stress is building up, and be kind to yourself – take breaks, breathe, and return to the present moment.

- **Polyvagal theory in practice.** We thrive when we connect. Co-regulation, exchanging safety signals with others, is essential for managing stress and building resilience. Let yourself be anchored by the shared moments of support, compassion, and care – these bonds strengthen our ability to weather life's storms.

- **Strategies to strengthen your well-being.** Small acts of self-care are powerful. Whether it is a comforting breath, a gentle stretch or a moment of laughter, these practices shape a life of vitality and inner peace.

- **Embrace mindfulness as a daily practice.** Mindfulness helps regulate responses to stress, creating a space to pause, reflect, and choose how we engage with challenges. Mindfulness is a journey, not a destination. Embrace each day as a chance to grow closer to yourself, grounding yourself in the present and unfolding your unique path.

Chapter 4
Play from a Polyvagal Theory Perspective

"We don't stop playing because we grow old;
we grow old because we stop playing."
– George Bernard Shaw

Amid our busy lives – navigating the complexities of remote work, juggling the demands of new motherhood or managing high-pressure responsibilities – it is easy to see ourselves as mere cogs in a machine. We become absorbed in the daily grind, focused solely on productivity and outcomes, often losing sight of our true essence. Yet here is a gentle reminder: We are not mechanical entities programmed for relentless work. At our core, we are living, breathing beings with an innate need for spontaneity, connection and joy.

Spontaneity isn't just about how we act but how we speak, think and engage with ourselves. It includes our inner dialogue or the way we talk to ourselves. Our voice is an embodied experience. Reflect for a moment on how you speak to yourself:

Is it with compassion and love, or are you often critical? In moments when things don't go as planned – whether you miss a deadline, face conflict, or encounter other challenges – kindness in your self-talk can make all the difference. Spontaneity invites openness, allowing for unplanned, authentic responses to experiences and interactions, bringing freshness, creativity and freedom. By breaking from routine and embracing the present moment, we enhance our ability to adapt, explore new possibilities and nurture creativity, connection and emotional resilience. In this way, spontaneity encourages us to respond naturally and fully to the world around us, with kindness towards ourselves and others.

When you observe children at play, what do you notice? Their boundless curiosity, their eagerness to ask questions, touch everything and explore every corner of their world. They run, laugh and move with freedom untouched by worry. A child is fully immersed in each moment, unhindered by concerns about what others might think or how they appear. If they stumble and fall, they may cry briefly, but more often than not, they get up, dust themselves off and dive right back into play, never dwelling on the mishap.

Unlike us adults, who are often self-critical and focused on control, children are free from these inhibitions. They naturally embrace spontaneity and openness, allowing them to discover, adapt and connect with their surroundings in refreshingly authentic ways. This is the beauty of a child's play – they remind us of the freedom in living without filters, finding joy in the simple act of being present. In witnessing their play, we glimpse a profound lesson: Life can be lighter, less controlled and infinitely more joyful when we approach it with the same wonder.

When we consider play through the lens of polyvagal theory, we understand that it is a vital component of our well-being, embedded in our mental and emotional health. Engaging in playful activities – whether taking a brief creative break, sharing a light-hearted game with colleagues, or participating in a personal hobby – activates the ventral vagal state of our nervous system. This state, marked by feelings of calm, safety, and social connectedness, counterbalances the stress and tension that often accompanies demanding work.

Understanding Polyvagal Theory

- **The ventral vagal state** is associated with social engagement, calmness, and connection. Play activates this state.

- **The sympathetic state** is linked to the fight-or-flight response, often triggered by stress and high demands.

- **The dorsal vagal state** is related to shut-down and immobilisation in the face of extreme stress or danger. Unable to play.

Our nervous system continuously shifts between these states in response to our environment. For office and remote workers, understanding these states can be transformative in managing stress and nurturing well-being.

The Role of Play in the Ventral Vagal State

Play is a vital, enlivening force in our lives, especially for working professionals who are often weighed down by the relentless demands of deadlines, meetings and responsibilities. It invites us to break from routine and respond to the present moment with authenticity and openness, creating opportunities to reconnect with ourselves and others. Play activates the ventral vagal state, where we feel calm, centred and socially connected[1] – a state essential for genuine connection that often gets buried in the rush of modern work culture. Engaging in spontaneous, playful moments – whether through laughter, a light-hearted joke or a creative exercise – opens a space for collaboration and connection. In these moments, we feel safe sharing and exploring, deepening our relationships and building a sense of support.

Children embody spontaneity so naturally, expressing their emotions without hesitation. When they are happy, they laugh, run and light up the space around them; when they are angry, they show it without suppressing their feelings. They fully experience each emotion, free from the self-conscious restraint that often hinders adults. Conversely, adults tend to hide or repress these emotions, often out of a cultural or social need to maintain control or appear composed. Western society often emphasises a linear, logical and left-brained approach, while some cultures value a more emotional and experiential perspective. The goal is to cultivate and balance both, achieving harmony and homeostasis. While these tendencies can vary widely across cultures, the inclination to restrain rather than release feelings is common in many adult lives. Yet embracing spontaneity allows us to reconnect with the essence of childlike play – to feel joy more fully, express ourselves freely and experience the natural ebb and flow of emotions. Doing so brings a sense of lightness and creativity back into our lives, allowing us to approach each day with curiosity, resilience and a renewed capacity for connection.

One of the key benefits of play is its ability to stimulate creativity. When we allow ourselves to engage playfully, our brains become more flexible, leading to innovative thinking and problem-solving.

I've noticed in my own life that when I become rigid or stressed, ideas tend to dry up. But when I give myself permission to be playful, whether through playing an instrument, brainstorming or even a quick, creative exercise, the ideas start flowing effortlessly.

Play frees up mental space, opening pathways for fresh insights and helping us approach challenges with renewed energy. Perhaps most importantly, play is a powerful antidote to stress, a force many battle daily. When caught up in the intensity of work, our nervous system often shifts into the sympathetic (stress) state, triggering that all-too-familiar fight-or-flight response. If this state persists, it can lead to burnout, anxiety and a sense of overwhelm. But play can interrupt that cycle. It helps shift the nervous system from the sympathetic state into the more relaxed ventral vagal state, where we feel grounded and present. Even small moments of play – like stepping outside for a walk, sharing a fun conversation with a colleague or taking a playful pause – can reset both the body and mind, releasing tension and restoring balance.

For example, stepping away for just five minutes to engage in something playful can make all the difference if you are in the middle of a stressful day at work. It could be as simple as chatting with a co-worker, stretching or even playing with a stress ball at your desk. I introduced one of my clients to use a stress ball, as he wasn't quite ready to commit to exercise or nutrition. I had to meet him where he was, and a simple play with the stress ball turned out to be something that worked for him. It helped him manage stress by releasing kinetic energy, and as a bonus, he got a light arm and hand workout at the same time.

These small, playful moments can have a significant impact, especially when the bigger steps seem overwhelming. They can also help break the cycle of stress and give you the mental clarity needed to approach tasks more effectively. It is easy to think we don't have time for play, but the reality is that these moments are what recharge us, preventing burnout and encouraging a healthier, more sustainable work-life homeostasis.

I have witnessed many professionals, including myself, hit points of exhaustion because we don't permit ourselves to play. We get caught in the trap of thinking that every moment must be productive and that if we step away, we are somehow falling behind. But the truth is, play is one of the most productive things we can do for our well-being. Whether it is taking a few minutes to doodle, listening to a song that lifts your spirits or engaging in a light-hearted challenge with a colleague, these moments shift us out of that high-stress state and back into a place of calm and creativity. By embracing play, even in small doses throughout the day, we reduce stress and create space for renewed energy, fresh ideas and deeper social bonds. Ultimately, play isn't just a luxury – it is an essential tool for maintaining balance, building resilience and stimulating a more fulfilling, creative work life.

Below are a few helpful exercises from Deb Dana's book *Polyvagal Exercises for Safety and Connection: 50 Client-Centered Practices.*[2]

Exercises

Exercise 1:

When you think about play, what is your autonomic response?

Play is _____

Exercise 2:

Where, when and with whom does your sense of playfulness emerge?

When, where and with whom does your sense of playfulness disappear? What states are activated?

What are the conditions that make play safe for you?

Each exercise invites you to explore your relationship with play, helping you understand the conditions that create a sense of safety, ease and openness. Through these reflections, you can gain insight into how playfulness affects your autonomic response, the environments and relationships that support it and the states that may either encourage or inhibit it. These prompts are designed to bring awareness to your unique play experiences, helping you reconnect with this vital, spontaneous part of yourself.

Benefits of Play for Remote Workers

Remote workers face unique challenges, especially when it comes to isolation and loneliness. Without the daily interactions that naturally occur in an office setting, it is easy for remote workers to feel disconnected. Play can serve as an antidote to this, helping to maintain social connections even when physically apart. Whether through virtual games, light-hearted check-ins or shared activities, play can bring people together meaningfully. I've seen teams that integrate regular virtual games or group travels thrive in ways that remote workers who feel isolated do not. When teams play together, even in a virtual setting, they create stronger bonds, which boosts morale and collaboration.

One of my clients, Paul, who runs a successful business, found a unique way to incorporate play into his life. After suffering serious health issues some years ago, Paul reconnected with his passion for singing. What started as a playful hobby eventually became a secondary career alongside his business. Singing not only brings him immense joy but also serves as an outlet for his creativity and emotional well-being.

Now, he is thriving in both worlds and even mentors me on using my voice, offering exercises for voice clarity and expression. Paul's playful approach to life reminds me – and others – that embracing joy into our day can be both enriching and energising. His journey with singing is an excellent example of how play can open doors to unexpected paths and give us renewed energy for both work and life.

This also brings us to motivation. Incorporating play into your workday can increase your motivation and job satisfaction. It can also make remote work more enjoyable and sustainable in the long run.

Finally, play helps remote workers establish a better work-life balance. When your work and home life occupy the same space, it can be challenging to switch off from work. Play creates a natural boundary, signalling when it is time to unwind and enjoy personal time. This doesn't have to be complicated. It could be a quick game, a hobby you love or spending time with loved ones.

Paul, for example, balances running his business with his passion for singing, which provides him with joy and helps him create that separation between work and relaxation. This joy then radiates into other areas of his life, energising and empowering him to approach challenges with renewed focus and enthusiasm. By embracing play in whatever form feels right, you can find a rhythm that makes you feel more connected, motivated and balanced.

Personal Reflections on Play

Lately, I have been asking myself, "How do I play"? and "How do I play with others?" Even though much of my work taps into creative energy, I often feel that flow gets restricted. As perfectionists, we tend to keep things under control, tightly scheduled and meticulously managed, believing professionalism means sticking to a certain rigidity and fitting into societal expectations. Of course, having a moral compass, acting ethically and being accountable are all important – but where does that leave space for playfulness? How do we keep the fun and joy alive when our days are filled with endless tasks?

The mind can work overtime to distract us, especially when we lack purpose or connection. When disconnected from our true selves or our goals feel unclear, we often turn to distractions for comfort or escape. It is easy to slip into habits that fill the time – bingeing Netflix, scrolling on social media, having a drink or two after work, or overindulging on the weekends. I have been there too. These moments might feel like rest, but they rarely leave us truly refreshed or nourished.

It took some honest reflection to realise that those distractions weren't the play or enjoyment I needed – they were a way of numbing or avoiding that feeling of being "stuck." Shifting my focus back to mindful, simple pleasures – cooking a meal from scratch, taking a walk without my phone, or just playing with new ideas in my journal – has helped me reconnect with a deeper sense of joy. It is a reminder that play doesn't have to be extravagant. It is often found in the small, intentional moments where we permit ourselves just to be. When we allow ourselves to loosen the grip of perfectionism, we can rediscover the fun that has always been there, waiting.

Further reflecting on my journey, I remember the early days of building my business. I was overwhelmed by tasks like developing a business plan, setting up a website and managing social media. Tech wasn't my strong suit, and honestly, it frustrated me to no end. The fear of making mistakes took all the fun out of the process. It wasn't until I reached out for support and built a team that shared my vision that things began to change.

Allowing myself to focus on my strengths while trusting others with their expertise turned the process into a playful and productive journey. What once seemed like a chore became a space to weave my creative energy into something meaningful and enjoyable. I also learned to delegate tasks, communicate my vision and trust others to share it. I learned to play with others.

For every business owner and professional, having trustworthy and supportive people in their circle is crucial, not just for the success of their business but also for their overall well-being. When you are surrounded by people who genuinely want you to succeed, guide you and hold space for your growth, it creates an environment where you can thrive. This trust deepens social connections and builds a safe foundation, allowing you to explore new ideas and take risks confidently.

Having that kind of safe space, where your circle truly supports and believes in you, is incredibly empowering. They encourage you to be the best version of yourself, to push through challenges and to step into opportunities you may have doubted.

When I am in the company of those who genuinely care about my success and well-being, it opens up much more room for creativity and collaboration. It is as though you are being held, not just by their belief in you, but by a shared commitment to growth and possibility - it feels safe and nurturing.

It is worth taking the time to nurture those relationships, give and receive support, and surround yourself with people who help you feel safe enough to take risks and be playful in your work. Trust that these connections will elevate your career and your sense of purpose and joy in what you do.

This experience led me to a deeper question about what truly drives us. Is it passion, joy or the fear of not being enough? When our actions are motivated by external validation or a sense of lack, they can feel rigid and stifling, overshadowing the spontaneous joy that once came naturally. Peeling back the layers of our motivations – like peeling an onion – can help us uncover the deeper energies driving our actions.

While working with a client, I noticed an artwork on her wall with a quote that resonated deeply with me: *"If you want to achieve greatness, stop asking for permission."* That quote struck a chord, and it now hangs on my vision board as a daily reminder to embrace my potential without hesitating to seek external validation. Reconnecting with this child-like sense of wonder and abundance is a process that takes time, but it is essential for living authentically and joyfully.

As silly as it might sound, it took me a while to realise that writing this book was an opportunity to tap into my creative energy. While there was undeniable excitement and pride in the process, I found myself so focused on producing material that I forgot to enjoy the journey. I had to step back and do deep, introspective work to open up those creative channels. Breath work and somatic therapy proved incredibly valuable guidance in this process, helping me connect with my deeper emotions.

During this introspective work, I unearthed some underlying fears – fear of rejection and criticism and many "what ifs." "What if I present myself this way and people think less of me?" and similar anxieties bubbled to the surface.

Going further, I realised that this fear of rejection sometimes manifested as people-pleasing. People-pleasing comes from feeling "less" rather than recognising our inherent "more." It is driven by a sense of inadequacy rather than self-acceptance. In acknowledging this, I made a conscious decision to love myself through this journey of self-discovery and to express that self-love and openness through my writing.

This experience is profoundly relevant to working profession-als. Many of us face similar pressures in our work environments – the constant push to achieve, the fear of criticism, or the ten-dency to people-please to fit in or seek approval. We often get so caught up in meeting external expectations and maintaining a facade of professionalism that we forget to enjoy our work and tap into our creative potential.

Integrating practices like breathwork or other self-reflective techniques into your routine can help you address these un-derlying fears and pressures. Recognising and embracing your strengths and vulnerabilities can shift your approach from rigidity and stress to openness and creativity. This shift improves productivity and nurtures a more fulfilling and enjoyable work experience.

Don't be afraid to be authentic and spontaneous. Embracing your true self, rather than striving for perfection or seeking external validation, can lead to greater satisfaction and a more balanced work-life dynamic.

As you navigate your professional responsibilities, remember that self-compassion and authenticity aren't just personal values – they are powerful guides for thriving in any work environment. By embracing your imperfections and nurturing your creative energy, you allow yourself to enjoy the journey, much like I learned in my own process.

Remember learning to ride a bike? Those first few attempts were far from playful – more like a series of tumbles, scraped knees and frustration. Yet, once you got the hang of it, riding became a joy. Similarly, when we let go of perfectionism and embrace our imperfections, we rediscover what it means to truly play. We begin to see that playfulness isn't the opposite of professionalism – it is an essential part of it.

Reflection

Take a moment to recall the joyful moments from your childhood. Was it building sandcastles, dancing, singing, creating a treehouse, or something else that filled you with excitement and wonder? Write these memories down and reflect on how you can reconnect with that child-like energy and creativity in your life today. Consider how these simple joys inspire you to approach challenges with curiosity and playfulness.

As you explore the ideas in this book, I encourage you to approach them with a blend of responsibility and playfulness. Embrace the process with an open heart and a willingness to experiment. It is easy to forget, but your nervous system will guide you – showing you where you feel safe to be playful and in which situations you can let your guard down. Trust that inner wisdom.

Befriend your nervous system and have that conversation - it knows more than we often give it credit for. By doing so, you'll find new ways to unlock your creativity, deepen your connections with others and create a more balanced, fulfilling life.

Joy and spontaneity aren't just luxuries but essential for our well-being. When we tune into the signals our body sends us, we can recognise when it is okay to relax and play. I have learned that trusting those moments makes it easier to lean into fun without feeling guilty or like I need to constantly be "on."

So, let us lean into this energy together. Trust the process, listen to what your body tells you and give yourself permission to have fun along the way. Playfulness doesn't need to be forced – it is already within you, waiting for the right moment to emerge. When embraced, those moments can transform not just your work but your entire approach to life.

Key Points

- **The importance of play in well-being.** Engaging in playful moments can relieve stress, spark creativity and encourage a sense of connection, making play a valuable tool for resilience and joy.

- **Activating the ventral vagal state through play.** Play activates the ventral vagal state, creating feelings of safety, calm and connection. This state supports healthy social interactions, reduces stress and creates a mental space where professionals can approach challenges with creativity and openness.

- **Breaking the cycle of stress with spontaneity.** Embracing spontaneity allows us to break free from rigid routines and stressful patterns, encouraging a more adaptive and responsive approach to life. We can recharge and foster mental clarity by letting go of constant productivity demands, reducing burnout.

- **Play as a remedy for remote work isolation.** For remote workers, play can alleviate isolation and increase motivation. Engaging in playful interactions, even virtually, strengthens bonds and cultivates a supportive work environment, helping remote workers feel more connected and present.

- **Embracing imperfections for authenticity and joy.** Overcoming perfectionism and people-pleasing fosters authentic self-expression and reduces stress. Embracing imperfections allows professionals to engage more fully in their work and life, finding joy and satisfaction rather than striving for unreachable standards.

- **Building social connections for well-being.** A supportive circle enhances resilience and creativity by providing a safe space to explore, take risks and connect authentically. Trusted relationships help us feel anchored, valued and empowered to grow personally and professionally.

Chapter 5
Purposeful Progress: Shaping Goals with Mindfulness

"Do something today that your future self will thank you for."
– Sean Patrick Flanery

In today's fast-paced world, where the lines between work and personal life often blur – especially for those working from home – mindful goal setting has never been more important. Traditional goal-setting methods typically emphasise productivity and achievement above all else, driving us to tick boxes without leaving room for reflection, harmony or well-being. For professionals navigating the demands of office life or adapting to remote work environments, this relentless pursuit of productivity can lead to a perpetual state of busyness, lacking a true sense of fulfilment or purpose.

Mindful goal setting shifts the focus from merely completing tasks to setting intentions that genuinely align with your core values, personal aspirations and overall well-being. It invites you to be fully present in defining what success means for you rather than following external expectations. By incorporating mindfulness into your goal-setting process, you create the space to pause, reflect and connect with what truly matters, allowing you to set goals that feel meaningful and sustainable rather than just another item on an endless to-do list. Thoughtfully setting intentions creates room for balance, resilience and a more fulfilling connection to both your work and life.

This approach is particularly relevant in today's work landscape, where stress, burnout and the constant pressure to perform can significantly affect our mental and physical health. For those working from home, the absence of clear boundaries can easily blur work and personal time, often leading to overworking and a growing sense of disconnection from both work and self. Mindful goal setting provides a pathway for professionals to create a more sustainable and intentional relationship with their work, encouraging focus, resilience and overall satisfaction. Setting goals honouring productivity and well-being creates a work environment supporting sustainable success rather than exhaustion. This mindful approach to goal setting encourages you to prioritise self-care alongside achievement, creating space for a more fulfilling and grounded work experience.

When you bring mindfulness into the goal-setting process, you are not just planning your next steps – you are honouring the state of your nervous system. This chapter builds upon the foundations in previous discussions on polyvagal theory, mindfulness and the importance of play. The polyvagal theory teaches us that our nervous system's state greatly influences our ability to feel safe, connected and engaged. When we are stuck in a constant state of fight-or-flight, our capacity to think

clearly, make sound decisions and work effectively is significantly diminished. As explored earlier, mindfulness helps us
become aware of these states, giving us the tools to self-regu-
late and bring ourselves back into a calmer, more engaged state
where we can perform at our best. Mindful goal setting is about
more than just achieving results; it is about aligning your goals
with your inner state and creating a rhythm that supports rather than depletes you.

By recognising when you need to push forward and when you
need to pause, you can navigate challenges with greater ease
and adaptability. Setting nervous system-friendly goals that
challenge but don't overwhelm you helps keep you grounded, engaged and motivated. Remaining flexible is important,
as circumstances can change, new opportunities can arise and
a playful mindset allows you to navigate these shifts with creativity and fresh ideas. This approach brings moments of spontaneity and joy into your routines – powerful tools for resetting
your nervous system and reigniting your creativity.

Without clear goals and planning, we all may find ourselves lost
in a sea of unstructured tasks, leading to missed deadlines, reduced job satisfaction and a significant drop in motivation and
well-being. Research shows the negative effects of goal misfir-
ing on self-esteem and motivation, highlighting the importance
of structured yet mindful goal setting.[1] Effective goal setting is
essential whether you are a seasoned remote worker, a frequent
traveller or a traditional office professional transitioning to a
hybrid model. It provides a framework for organising priorities,
maintaining focus and measuring progress towards your objectives. For working professionals, goal setting is not just about

efficiency; it is about aligning daily tasks with broader career aspirations, improving job satisfaction and encouraging continuous growth. In today's dynamic work landscape, unforeseen circumstances and sudden changes are common, whether due to organisational shifts, personal life events or evolving work requirements. My clients who are remote workers or entrepreneurs often share how they face last-minute events, unexpected changes and shifting priorities.

For them, staying flexible with their goals is crucial, allowing them to adjust smoothly without feeling derailed. Flexibility in goal setting also enables them to embrace new opportunities and pivot effectively, turning challenges into growth experiences. A mindful, adaptable approach to goal setting keeps them grounded and aligned with their purpose, even in unpredictable situations.

"People often say that motivation doesn't last. Well, neither does bathing – that's why we recommend it daily."
– Zig Ziglar

Many techniques are available for setting and managing goals – such as SMART goals, priority matrices, vision boards, reflection journals and planners, some of which we have discussed in previous chapters. These tools can be invaluable, especially for remote work, helping you stay on track and maintain balance. Depending on their needs, I always recommend that clients take a mix-and-match approach with these techniques. Sometimes, you might want to combine two or three methods, while other times, focusing on just one approach can help you break down a complex goal into manageable steps. This process is not about rigidly sticking to a single method but finding what resonates and feels right for you in each moment. Different techniques resonate with different people and that is perfectly okay. The aim here isn't to convince you which method to use but to encourage you to explore and experiment with them all. See what fits your style and be open to switching things up when needed. What is most important is the motivation behind the goal itself – your intention, your "why" and how it connects to your values. The tools support you, but the heart of the process lies in your commitment to staying present, adapting and honouring your unique journey towards success.

Steps to Achieve Meaningful and Sustainable Success

Achieving meaningful and sustainable success goes beyond simply ticking boxes or reaching milestones. This practice is about creating a journey that aligns with your values, purpose and well-being. In a world that prioritises fast results, it can be easy to overlook the importance of thoughtful goal-setting and mindful progression. These steps provide a roadmap to help you approach your goals with intention, alignment and adaptability. Each step encourages you to connect deeply with your purpose, set goals that support rather than overwhelm you and incorporate practices that bring joy and flexibility to the process.

Embracing mindful accountability along the way ensures you are moving forward and appreciating the journey itself. By following these steps, you will start creating a sense of fulfilment and resilience, making your success both achievable and meaningful.

Step 1: Connect With Your "Why"

Understanding the deeper purpose behind your goals is foundational to setting intentions that truly resonate with you. Take a moment to pause and reflect: Why does this goal matter to you personally? Is it aligned with your core values, or are you pursuing it because of external expectations or pressures? Mindfulness plays an important role here. By taking a few deep breaths and checking in with yourself, you can connect with your intrinsic motivations and gain clarity on what drives you.

I have found that when I truly understand my "why," even the most daunting tasks become meaningful. This connection fuels your motivation and provides a sense of purpose that guides you through challenging times. It is like having a personal compass that keeps you oriented towards what genuinely matters. If you lack clarity on your "why," your goals can start to feel empty or burdensome, making it harder to stay motivated and engaged, especially when challenges arise.

Without a clear purpose, it is easy to become distracted by others' expectations or to lose sight of what truly matters to you. When your goals reflect your deepest values, they become more than mere tasks; they transform into a journey that aligns with your true self and brings genuine fulfilment.

Prompt Questions

- What personal values or beliefs make this goal meaningful to me?

Reflect on how this goal aligns with what matters most to you.

- How will achieving this goal positively impact my life and those around me?

    Consider how this goal resonates beyond the outcome, bringing a sense of purpose and connection.

- Am I pursuing this goal for myself, or am I influenced by others' expectations?

    Take a moment to explore whether this goal reflects your own aspirations or is shaped by external pressures.

Step 2: Set Nervous System-Friendly Goals

Our nervous system responds to stress in ways that can hinder our progress if we are not mindful. When setting goals, it is important to consider how they impact your emotional and physiological state. Goals that are too ambitious or numerous can overwhelm your nervous system, causing anxiety or a sense of being stuck. When your goals aren't nervous system-friendly, this stress can lead to burnout, decreased motivation and even avoidance of the tasks altogether. Instead of feeling inspired, you may find yourself procrastinating or feeling paralysed by the demands you have set.

To prevent this, break your goals down into smaller, manageable steps. Each step should be challenging yet achievable, allowing you to experience a sense of accomplishment as you progress. Celebrating these small wins keeps your nervous system regulated, making it easier to stay engaged and motivated.

From my experience, approaching goals in incremental stages makes them feel more attainable and helps maintain a steady flow of motivation. Each small victory builds confidence and reinforces your commitment, making the overall journey less daunting and more manageable.

It is also important not to multitask – dividing your attention dilutes your focus and reduces the quality of your efforts. By concentrating on one task at a time, you can give it your full energy and remain present, making progress faster and more effective.

Prompt Questions

- Is this goal achievable in its current form, or can I break it down into smaller steps?

  Reflect on how you can simplify the goal to make it feel manageable and less overwhelming.

- How does thinking about this goal make me feel physically and emotionally?

  Take a moment to tune into your body's response. Do you feel calm, motivated or tense? This awareness can help you adjust your goal to be more supportive.

- Am I focusing on one step at a time, or am I trying to tackle everything at once?

  For a more focused and relaxed approach, consider slowing down, concentrating on one task and taking it one step at a time.

Step 3: Incorporate Play and Flexibility

Incorporating moments of play and flexibility into your routine is vital for maintaining balance and creativity. Play isn't just a childhood activity; it is an essential part of adult life that helps reduce stress and stimulate creativity. Allowing yourself time for spontaneous activities and light-hearted moments allows your nervous system to reset and rejuvenate. Flexibility is particularly crucial in remote work or entrepreneurship, where circumstances can shift rapidly, often requiring fast decisions and adaptability.

Without play and flexibility in your goal setting, the journey can become overly rigid and exhausting, making it harder to adapt when things don't go as planned. This rigidity often leads to burnout, diminished creativity and a loss of joy in the process, as you become fixated on ticking off tasks rather than engaging with them meaningfully.

I recall a period when I was deeply immersed in achieving my goals, only to feel drained and uninspired. It wasn't until I took a break and spent a weekend with a close friend and her daughter, enjoying good food and relaxed conversations, that I felt revitalised. There is something about being in the presence of a child – their pure joy, curiosity and playfulness – that reminds us of a lighter, more effortless energy. It is a powerful reset, a reminder that sometimes, reconnecting with the simple, unfiltered delight of childhood restores us in ways we least expect.

Play and flexibility aren't just about taking breaks; they are about giving yourself permission to enjoy the process and remain open to change. This mindset helps you approach your goals with renewed energy and fresh perspectives, ensuring that your journey remains enjoyable, adaptable and fulfilling.

Prompt Questions

- What activities bring joy and help me feel refreshed, even for a few minutes?

  Reflect on ways to incorporate these light-hearted moments into your routine to maintain a sense of ease and creativity.

- How can I build flexibility into my goals so I can adapt if circumstances change?

  Consider what adjustments might allow for a more fluid approach, helping you stay engaged and avoid feeling stuck if plans need to shift.

- Am I giving myself permission to enjoy the journey, or am I solely focused on the end result?

  Take a moment to assess whether you are creating space for play and enjoyment along the way, allowing each step to feel meaningful and fulfilling.

Step 4: Practice Mindful Accountability

Mindful accountability is about assessing your progress with a compassionate and reflective mindset. Rather than fixating on perfection, approach your evaluations with curiosity and kindness. Take a moment to check in: How do you feel about your progress? Are there any adjustments that could better support your journey? This practice encourages you to recognise and celebrate even small achievements while addressing challenges with a gentle attitude. I have found that being mindful of my progress and reflecting on setbacks with self-compassion keeps me both motivated and focused.

If you don't practice mindful accountability, it is easy to become overly critical of yourself, focusing on what hasn't been done rather than acknowledging the progress you have made. This can lead to discouragement, self-doubt and even a tendency to give up on goals that once felt meaningful.

As Henry David Thoreau wisely said, *"Success usually comes to those who are too busy to be looking for it."* This reminds us that true success is achieved by engaging fully with the process rather than fixating solely on the end goal. It is about being present, putting in consistent effort and immersing yourself in each step along the way.

When you focus on growth, learning and meaningful progress, success becomes a natural outcome of your dedication and presence. By recognising your accomplishments and openness to change, you develop a positive, resilient mindset that keeps you moving forward. This approach keeps you on track and endorses gratitude and a deeper appreciation for your unique path.

Prompt Questions

- How do I feel about my progress so far?

Reflect on your emotions surrounding your journey, acknowledging both accomplishments and areas where you may want to adjust.

- What small achievements can I celebrate today, and how can I show myself appreciation for my efforts?

  Take a moment to recognise the wins, no matter how small, and honour your commitment to your goals.

- Are there any adjustments I could make that would support me better in achieving my goals?

  Consider whether a change in approach might make your journey more fulfilling, allowing for both growth and flexibility as you move forward.

Staying flexible is necessary in today's dynamic work environment. Be prepared to adapt your goals and action plans based on new circumstances, opportunities or feedback. From my training with Debra and Robert Maldonado at Creative Mind University, I learned the three key elements of success: clarity, consistency and intensity.

1. **Clarity** helps you focus on what truly matters and is essential for directing your energy toward meaningful goals that align with your values and purpose. Without clarity, it is easy to feel scattered or overwhelmed, pursuing goals that may not truly serve you or falling into patterns driven by external pressures rather than genuine motivation. This lack of focus can lead to frustration, indecision and even burnout as you expend effort on tasks that ultimately don't fulfil or advance your aspirations. Clarity helps you prioritise ef-

fectively, making each step intentional and purpose-driven, which empowers you to make decisions confidently and stay on course.

2. **Consistency** is about showing up, even when motivation fades. It is crucial for building momentum and steadily progressing toward your goals. Lack of consistency can make you lose direction or get derailed by distractions, leading to stalled progress and a lack of measurable results. When you don't show up regularly, even small setbacks can feel overwhelming, and you may lose confidence or begin to doubt your ability to succeed. Developing habits and routines supporting your goals helps bridge the gap between short-term motivation and long-term achievement, ensuring that you continue moving forward, even when motivation is low.

3. **Intensity** is about the depth of commitment, passion and energy you bring to your goals, pushing yourself beyond your comfort zone to achieve impactful results. Without intensity, you may approach tasks with minimal effort, leading to mediocre outcomes and a lack of real progress. When you invest fully and focus on high-impact activities, you can apply Pareto's Principle – recognising that *80% of your results will often come from 20% of your efforts directed toward what truly matters.* Channelling your energy into this critical 20% enables you to achieve meaningful, lasting success rather than spreading yourself too thin across low-value tasks.

I encourage you to reflect on what might be draining your energy and keeping you from your goals at the moment. Sometimes, these drains can be subtle, like habits or routines that no longer serve you or negative self-talk that saps your motivation. Identify and address those distractions, and seek feedback from mentors or trusted peers, using their insights to refine your approach. By intentionally letting go of what no longer aligns with your goals, you will free up valuable energy, creating space to focus on what truly matters and move forward with clarity and strength.

Practice celebrating your progress, no matter how small, as it reinforces positive habits and motivates you for the next steps. This mindset of gratitude and appreciation enriches your journey and encourages you to extend that celebration to others, creating a supportive culture of success. Remember, feeling overwhelmed or questioning your path is a natural part of the process. Progress ebbs and flows, and at times, you might feel alone or unsure.

Everyone's journey has its own rhythm, so surround yourself with trusted, honest and positive people who support and challenge you. I often think of Denzel Washington's quote: *"If you hang around five confident people, you'll be the 6th. If you hang around five intelligent people, you'll be the 6th. If you hang around five millionaires, you'll be the 6th. If you hang around five idiots, you'll be the 6th. Be smart!"* Your environment shapes you, so choose wisely. These relationships will help you step out of your head, navigate overwhelming moments, and empower your journey forward with renewed strength and purpose.

Mindful goal setting isn't just about productivity. This approach is about being kind to yourself in the process. Many of my clients who face increasingly high stress levels have shared that they often feel compelled to multitask, juggling numerous goals – some of which are overly ambitious. This relentless pressure can lead to burnout, as they try to accomplish everything at once, often without a clear sense of what is truly meaningful to them.

Others struggle with perfectionism and a need for control, which can keep them stuck, fearing mistakes and unable to move forward. It is easy to get caught up in the drive to accomplish everything quickly, but there is real wisdom in pacing yourself and staying present with each step. For these clients, mindful goal setting has been a powerful tool to help break down goals into manageable steps, pacing themselves with intention rather than pressure. The approach encourages you to "eat the elephant one bite at a time," as my friend Stuart often reminds me, making even the most daunting challenges feel possible and rewarding.

This process helps you learn to appreciate the journey rather than focusing solely on the end result, understanding that progress is made in moments, not leaps. When you stay focused on each step, you bring greater ease and balance into your life and also transform overwhelming tasks into achievable, meaningful experiences.

Ultimately, mindful goal setting isn't just about achieving success; it is about crafting a path that aligns with your nervous system, prioritises self-care and gives you the freedom to pause, play and recalibrate as needed. This approach can be transformative for remote workers, in particular, who may face unique challenges such as blurred boundaries and a constant need for self-regulation. By setting nervous system-friendly goals, you build resilience, reduce stress and create a rhythm that respects your professional aspirations and personal well-being.

Integrating principles from polyvagal theory, mindfulness and play offers a holistic framework that allows you to stay grounded, adapt to changes and find joy in the journey. This compassionate and sustainable goal-setting approach equally honours your health, creativity and ambition, creating a healthy work-life rhythm and supporting long-term fulfilment and success.

Key Points

- Aligning goals with values and purpose. Mindful goal setting encourages connecting with your "why" to ensure goals resonate with your core values. This creates a journey that feels meaningful and fulfilling rather than simply task-driven.

- Setting nervous system-friendly goals. Goals should be ambitious yet achievable to prevent overwhelm. By breaking down large goals into manageable steps, you can maintain motivation and avoid burnout, creating a sustainable pace that respects your mental and physical well-being.

- Incorporating play and flexibility. Embracing play and flexibility within your goal setting allows room for spontaneity and joy, helping you stay adaptable and creative, especially when unexpected changes occur in the work environment.

- Practising mindful accountability. Regularly assessing progress with self-compassion creates resilience and gratitude. Mindful accountability allows for celebrating small wins and gentle course corrections, enhancing motivation and overall satisfaction.

- Staying flexible and open to change. In today's dynamic work environment. Adapting to new circumstances, feedback or opportunities ensures that goals remain relevant and achievable, promoting continuous growth and resilience.

- Creating a sustainable approach to success. Mindful goal setting integrates polyvagal theory, mindfulness and play, offering a balanced framework that honours personal well-being and professional success, ultimately supporting long-term fulfilment.

Chapter 6
Establishing a Sleep Routine and Optimising Sleep Quality

"Let her sleep, for when she wakes, she will move mountains."
— Napoleon Bonaparte

As we explored in the previous chapters, the polyvagal theory highlights the important role of our nervous system in regulating our emotional and physical responses. Mindfulness allows us to consciously tune into our bodies, recognising when we are stuck in states of stress and guiding ourselves back to calm and connection. However, there is another cornerstone of this regulation that often gets overlooked: *sleep.* Sleep is a fundamental yet frequently overlooked aspect of maintaining overall well-being in remote work, where boundaries between professional and personal life often blur. It is a vital process that supports our body's ability to reset, repair and regulate.

Just as mindfulness supports nervous system balance, quality sleep reinforces these restorative processes. However, sleep isn't just about quantity - the timing and rhythm of our sleep cycles, directed by an internal process called the "circadian rhythm," are equally important. This natural rhythm aligns our sleep-wake cycle with the 24-hour day, guiding the release of hormones like cortisol and melatonin to sustain energy and alertness. When our circadian rhythm is in balance, cortisol peaks in the morning to promote wakefulness, while melatonin rises in the evening to gently prepare us for restful sleep. In addition to cortisol and melatonin, many other hormones play a role in our circadian rhythm, with some peaking during the night and others decreasing to support various bodily functions. While light and darkness primarily influence this rhythm, other factors such as food intake, stress levels, physical activity, social environment and temperature also have an influence. When hormone levels fluctuate or fall out of sync, they can lead to sleep disturbances and impact overall well-being. Disruptions to our circadian rhythm – such as working late into the evening, exposure to artificial light or irregular sleep schedules – can impair sleep quality. Maintaining a consistent circadian rhythm can be especially challenging for remote workers, who may work across different time zones or have flexible hours.

The circadian rhythm affects our ability to fall asleep and influences our sleep's depth and restorative quality. Without this regularity, even when we achieve recommended hours, we may miss out on the benefits of deep sleep stages that support physical repair, memory consolidation and emotional processing. Inconsistent sleep patterns, therefore, don't just leave us fatigued – they disrupt our nervous system's ability to regulate effectively, undermining the stress-management capacities that both polyvagal theory and mindfulness aim to support. Inadequate or disrupted sleep also impairs our ability to manage stress effectively, leading to a cascade of adverse effects on both mental and physical health. When our sleep is poor, the sympathetic nervous system, often associated with the "fight or flight" response, can become more reactive, leaving us vulnerable to stress, irritability and anxiety. This heightened reactivity makes engaging the parasympathetic "rest and digest" state challenging, which is essential for recovery and resilience.

MIDNIGHT
24.00

21.00
MELATONIN SECRETION
STARTS

02.00
DEEPEST SLEEP

19.00
HIGHEST
BODY TEMPERATURE

04.30
LOWEST
BODY TEMPERATURE

CIRCADIAN
RHYTHM

18.30
HIGHEST
BLOOD PRESSURE

18.00

06.00

06.45
SHARPEST
BLOOD PRESSURE RISE

17.00
BEST MUSCLE STRENGTH
AND CARDIOVASCULAR
EFFICIENCY

07.30
MELATONIN SECRETION
STOPS

15.30
FASTEST
REACTION TIME

NOON
12.00

14.30
BEST
COORDINATION

10.00
HIGHEST
ALERTNESS

In essence, quality sleep, anchored by a steady circadian rhythm, serves as a foundation for our nervous system's resilience. For remote workers, embracing routines that support regular sleep – such as winding down with low lighting, avoiding screens an hour before bed, and waking at a consistent time – can create a structure that reinforces this rhythm. Some clients who struggled with falling asleep or experienced restless nights found relief by making small but meaningful adjustments. Instead of watching TV before bed, they turned to calming routines like listening to soft music or using candles to create a relaxing atmosphere.

Upon waking, rather than reaching for their phones or leaping out of bed, many now spend 10-15 minutes waking up gently, using this time to bring mindful awareness to their morning. Some clients use these first moments to meditate or visualise their intentions for the day. Just as mindfulness practices help us stay attuned to our internal states, respecting and honouring our circadian rhythm empowers us to align with our natural cycles, ultimately strengthening our capacity to manage stress and maintain well-being in both personal and professional aspects of life.

For instance, after consulting with a nutritionist, I replaced my morning coffee with lemon water and now enjoy coffee around 10 a.m. I discovered that having coffee first thing in the morning fluctuated my body's natural cortisol levels, either amplifying or masking its production. Since making this change, I have noticed significant improvements in my morning rhythm, digestion and sustained energy levels throughout the day. Minor adjustments like these can make a profound difference, helping us align our habits with our body's natural needs.

Staying late might seem like a normal routine if you work from home, especially while balancing family responsibilities or managing a new business. But it is worth considering how these late nights impact your day. It is tempting to push through late nights, squeeze in work whenever you can, or sacrifice rest to meet the endless demands of your time. You may schedule calls or meetings at all hours, determined to keep things moving and grow your business or career. At first, this might feel manageable, fuelled by adrenaline, passion and the excitement of new opportunities. But over time, the lack of sleep starts to catch up. You may start to feel exhausted, unmotivated and disconnected, struggling to keep up with the day's demands. You might find yourself needing naps during the day, doubting your abilities and feeling like you are constantly playing catch-up. Sleep deprivation affects how you feel and impacts your mood, decision-making, health and how well you connect with others. In those moments, it is easy to question yourself and lose touch with your usual drive and enthusiasm.

I have been there myself. In my case, I discovered that my fatigue wasn't just due to the late nights and early mornings – it turned out I had a severe Vitamin D deficiency that was making everything worse. My energy levels were at an all-time low, and I felt constantly drained. Once I got my blood tested and addressed this deficiency, I started feeling like myself again. My sleep improved, and my motivation and mental clarity returned. It was a reminder of how important it is to listen to your body and take care of your health, not just focus on the hours you are putting in. This experience taught me an important lesson: Sleep isn't just a box to tick – it is foundational to how we function. Poor sleep affects our overall sense of well-being, leaving us feeling disconnected and depleted. If you are in a similar situation, it is important to recognise that your sleep habits are deeply intertwined with your ability to perform effectively and maintain your health.

You will notice the difference once you start prioritising sleep and making adjustments – whether through a medical check-up, changing your diet, introducing high-quality supplements into your daily routine or simply setting better boundaries around your work hours. Better sleep sharpens your cognitive abilities, improves your mood and helps you approach your work and life more effectively and sustainably. The first step is to ask yourself: What might be causing my sleep problems? How can I move from feeling perpetually tired to achieving quality sleep and more energy? Knowing what is going on with your body gives you a clear starting point and allows you to focus on adjusting your habits, environment and/or nutrition.

Research underscores the profound consequences of poor sleep on remote workers and professionals. Chronic sleep deprivation disrupts the body's natural circadian rhythms, impairing cognitive function, decision-making and emotional regulation. For instance, a published study highlights that sleep deprivation is linked to an increased risk of mood disorders, such as depression and anxiety, which can severely impact job performance and interpersonal relationships.[1] Moreover, sleep deprivation has been shown to compromise immune function, making individuals more susceptible to illness – a critical concern for remote workers who rely on their health to maintain consistent productivity and engagement.[2]

If you are a parent working from home with small children, as some of my clients do, I completely understand that sleep can sometimes feel elusive and chaotic. Some of my clients struggle to balance managing work, looking after the kids and finding even a moment of rest for themselves. It is easy to feel guilty for not getting it all right, but being kind to yourself is key. A solid sleep routine isn't just for them but also for you. You deserve rest just as much as anyone else, and prioritising your sleep can have a ripple effect on your whole day. I have seen first-hand how even small changes can make a big difference. For some of my clients, it is about carving out just 10 minutes of quiet time before bed or asking for help when things get overwhelming. For others, it is about embracing the imperfections and understanding that some nights will still be disrupted, and that is part of the process. Accepting this with grace allows for a more balanced and compassionate approach to rest.

New mothers returning to work, especially those with babies waking up through the night, face unique challenges. Sleep might feel like a luxury, but even short, consistent rest can help you recharge. Lean on your support system when you can, and don't underestimate the power of a short nap or a moment of calm during your day. For those who travel frequently, adjusting to new time zones and disrupted routines can mess with sleep, metabolism and health. By prioritising strategies, we can combat the challenges of travel-related sleep disturbances and maintain our performance on the road.

Take William, one of my clients who travels internationally for work. He was deeply impacted by jet lag and nutritional challenges during his trips. Once he started preparing mindfully – incorporating physical activities like yoga and ensuring adequate nutrition before and after travel – his experience shifted. After returning, he prioritised rest and self-care, making his travels more manageable. Of course, there are still physical challenges like long hours on planes or carrying heavy bags, which we easily address in a session, but his overall health and well-being have improved tremendously with this more holistic approach.

William's experience shows that it is not about avoiding the challenges entirely but learning how to navigate them in a way that supports your well-being. It is not about having a perfect routine but finding one that works for you. You can maintain balance by making small, mindful adjustments, even in hectic schedules. Whether it is making sure the kids are settled before you start winding down, setting a cut-off time for work, mindfully planning your travels or finding ways to relax – even for a few moments – those small adjustments can help you wake up feeling more refreshed and ready to face the day. Remember, you are not alone in this, and taking care of your sleep is one of the best things you can do for yourself and your family.

Poor sleep doesn't just leave us tired the next day; it has lasting effects on our overall health. Long-term sleep deficits can significantly impact metabolic health, with research linking poor sleep to an increased risk of conditions like obesity and type 2 diabetes. When we don't get enough rest, hormones that regulate our appetite and glucose metabolism are thrown off, leading to weight gain and problems with glucose tolerance.[3] For professionals, particularly those working remotely, this might mean more sick days, reduced work efficiency and, in the long run, higher healthcare costs. But even on a day-to-day level, not getting enough sleep directly affects how we perform at work. Lack of rest diminishes cognitive functions like focus, memory and problem-solving. One published review shows that sleep deprivation impairs executive functions and increases the likelihood of mistakes and accidents, which obviously impacts productivity and job satisfaction.[4] This is especially important for remote workers, who may not have the structure of a traditional office environment. Without that direct supervision, it can be easy to overlook the gradual decline in performance, potentially leading to burnout or a feeling of being overwhelmed.

It is important to be aware of how sleep (or lack of it) plays into your professional lives. If you have ever felt foggy-headed in the middle of a meeting or noticed it is harder to concentrate after a bad night's sleep, it is your body's way of telling you that rest is needed. Understanding this connection can encourage you to prioritise sleep in a way that feels manageable, even if that means making small adjustments to routines. Recognising these patterns early on can help prevent the long-term effects while improving your day-to-day performance and well-being. Addressing sleep issues through strategies informed by polyvagal theory and mindful practices can help mitigate these negative effects.

Prioritising good sleep hygiene – such as maintaining a consistent sleep schedule, creating a calming bedtime routine and managing stress – can improve your overall well-being and productivity. By understanding the interplay between sleep, stress regulation and work performance, remote workers can take proactive steps to improve their sleep quality and, consequently, their professional effectiveness and health. For many, small changes can lead to profound improvements. Your body and mind deserve the chance to recharge fully so that you can bring your best self to everything you do. Sleep isn't just a luxury – it is essential to functioning at your best. It is about creating a balance that works for you, allowing you to grow your business, be present for your family, and, most importantly, take care of yourself.

So, let's examine some practical steps you can take to improve your sleep habits, optimise sleep quality and prioritise rest as part of your self-care routine.

Optimise Your Sleep: Practical Steps for Better Rest

Sleep is the foundation for everything we do – how we recharge physically, emotionally and mentally. Yet, in the hustle of daily life, sleep often gets pushed aside. This section is about creating simple, mindful routines that can help you rest more deeply and wake up truly refreshed. Think of these as gentle shifts: setting a consistent sleep schedule, creating a soothing bedtime ritual and making your environment a restful haven. These practices are about connecting with a rhythm that brings balance and resilience to your life. Whether juggling work, family or personal goals, prioritising sleep can be a beautiful act of self-care that helps you show up as your best self. By tuning into these habits, you are setting yourself up for days filled with more clarity, energy and ease.

1. Establish a Consistent Sleep Schedule

Maintaining a consistent sleep schedule – going to bed and waking up at the same time each day – helps regulate your body's internal clock and supports the release of key hormones like cortisol and melatonin. Setting up reminders throughout the evening can signal your brain that it is time to wind down, and creating a calming bedtime ritual can reinforce this routine. Simple activities like dimming the lights, reading, burning incense or listening to soft music prepare your mind and body for sleep, bringing consistency and tranquillity to your evenings. This is especially important for parents who might have children with their own unpredictable schedules. Even if your kids' bedtime is chaotic, having your own set routine can anchor your day and help you feel more grounded.

2. Create a Relaxing Bedtime Routine

Engaging in calming activities before bed, such as reading, taking a warm bath or practising relaxation techniques like deep breathing or meditation is essential for calming the nervous system and easing into restful sleep. These rituals help lower cortisol levels, signalling to your body that it is time to unwind and encourage the production of melatonin, the hormone that prepares us for deep sleep. My own routine includes an evening facial and hair treatment – a small act of self-care that helps me wind down. You might enjoy lighting candles, using scented oils or listening to soothing music. Whatever you choose, make it your moment to reward yourself with care and love. Avoid screens during this time; your work will still be there in the morning, and giving yourself permission to unwind is essential for true rest.

3. Optimise Your Sleep Environment

Few things are more frustrating than waking up on the couch with the TV blaring, feeling stiff and unrested. To ensure quality rest, turn your bedroom into a true sanctuary – comfortable, calming, quiet and inviting. A soothing sleep environment helps regulate the nervous system, allowing your body to unwind and prepare for restorative sleep. Investing in blackout curtains, a white noise machine, a night light projector or an eye mask can make a difference. This space should feel safe, peaceful and conducive to relaxation, becoming a place you can retreat to whenever you need to reconnect with calm. For new parents, the space may include a crib or gentle night light, but it is still possible to maintain a cosy, restful atmosphere for everyone.

4. Limit Exposure to Screens Before Bed

Blue light from screens disrupts melatonin production, delaying sleep onset and diminishing sleep quality. Try to switch off devices at least an hour before bed to allow your body's natural rhythms to settle. I will admit that I have been guilty of drifting off to something on my iPad, only to wake up tired, with burning eyes and a heavy head. Now, I have swapped screen time for calming music or a meditation practice to ease into sleep, and the difference is truly remarkable. Many of my clients have made similar changes and found that these small adjustments make a noticeable improvement in their rest.

5. Be Mindful of Daytime Naps

If you find yourself needing a nap during the day, aim to keep it short – 20 to 30 minutes – and try to avoid napping late in the afternoon. While naps can be wonderfully refreshing, longer or late naps may interfere with your night-time sleep. As a new parent or someone working from home, it is important to listen to your body, so if you are feeling drained after a long day or an early start, don't feel guilty about taking a brief rest. Honour what your body needs, but keep it gentle and mindful to support a restful night ahead.

6. Monitor and Improve Your Sleep Quality

Sleep-tracking apps or devices can be a valuable way to understand your unique sleep patterns, including time spent in deep sleep and REM stages. These tools offer helpful insights for those who enjoy a bit of tech and data. Tracking your sleep can reveal areas where small adjustments to your habits, environment or routines could make a difference. Some of my clients have also started using these apps, and they have found it fascinating to see their sleep patterns unfold. The goal isn't to strive for perfection but to build a greater awareness of what truly supports your rest and helps you feel your best.

7. Watch Your Diet and Hydration

What we eat and drink plays a key role in how easily we drift off and how refreshed we feel the next day. Food and timing are linked to our circadian rhythm, influencing hormones like insulin and cortisol, which affect sleep quality. Some of my clients noticed a big difference just by swapping late-night caffeine for herbal tea, finding they woke up more rested and alert. Try to avoid heavy meals and alcohol close to bedtime, as these can disrupt sleep. Instead, if you are feeling peckish in the evening, opt for a lighter snack like a handful of nuts or a piece of fruit – something easy on the stomach. Staying hydrated during the day is equally important, though it is best to limit fluids before bed to avoid those late-night trips to the bathroom. Small, mindful choices like these set you up for better rest, boosting both energy and focus the next day.

8. Engage in Regular Physical Activity

Exercise is a powerful ally for sleep, helping to regulate your body's internal clock, reduce stress, and enhance overall sleep quality. However, timing is important – high-intensity exercise too close to bedtime can release stimulating hormones like cortisol and adrenaline, making it harder to wind down. For a more restful transition to sleep, try gentler evening activities like yoga, stretching or a relaxed walk to help calm the nervous system. Regular physical activity, even in small amounts, improves sleep quality and boosts mood and energy levels, building resilience for the day ahead. Many of my clients have felt the benefits first-hand. One, in particular, who struggled with disrupted sleep due to stress, noticed significant improvement by adding light movement to his routine. These mindful adjustments can make a world of difference for both physical well-being and mental clarity.

9. Manage Stress and Anxiety

Stress is one of the biggest disruptors to restful sleep, as it triggers the release of hormones like cortisol and adrenaline, which keep the body alert and can make it challenging to settle into sleep. Practising stress-reduction techniques such as journaling, mindfulness or meditation before bed can help ease this response and create the calm needed for quality rest. Meditation, in particular, activates the body's relaxation response, lowering cortisol levels and encouraging a state of calm that is conducive to sleep. Many of my clients have noticed a marked improvement by simply incorporating five to ten minutes of mindful breathing or light meditation before bed, helping them fall asleep more easily and stay asleep throughout the night. For those balancing work, family or the demands of new parenthood, finding these small pockets of calm can be challenging but so rewarding. Even a few moments to centre yourself before bed can greatly improve sleep quality, helping you manage stress and sustain energy the next day.

10. Seek Professional Help if Needed

If sleep continues to be a struggle despite your best efforts, consider seeking professional support. Chronic sleep issues may sometimes signal underlying conditions such as sleep apnoea, anxiety or depression that require specialised care. A healthcare provider or sleep specialist can help identify these root causes and offer tailored solutions to enhance both your sleep and overall well-being. Remember, you don't have to navigate these challenges alone; sometimes, the most empowering step is reaching out for guidance that can truly transform your quality of life.

As you build a sleep routine and optimise the quality of your rest, remember that these practices are not just tasks on a checklist but nurturing rituals that support your health, energy and overall well-being. Prioritising sleep is essential whether you are working from home, navigating parenthood or managing a demanding professional life. You are actively investing in your mental and emotional health by establishing a consistent sleep schedule, setting up a relaxing bedtime routine, and managing screen time. The aim isn't perfection, it is about finding a rhythm that honours your needs and helps you recharge fully, allowing you to show up as your best self each day. Think of sleep as a powerful form of self-care that fuels your passions, strengthens resilience and uplifts your mood. When we connect the dots between sleep, mindfulness and the polyvagal theory, we see how these practices work harmoniously, fostering a balanced, resilient and fulfilling life.

Embrace these practices gently, and give yourself the gift of rest. By tuning into what helps you sleep best, you invest in your long-term health, empowering yourself for a life filled with clarity, energy and purpose.

Key Points

- **Understand the power of circadian rhythm and hormonal balance.** Aligning with your natural circadian rhythm stimulates hormones like cortisol and melatonin, which support wakefulness and sleep. Daily routines that follow this rhythm enhance sleep quality, mood and resilience.

- **Recognise the interplay between sleep and emotional well-being.** Quality sleep is vital for emotional stability and stress resilience. Deep sleep stages support physical recovery and mental health, helping you approach life with a grounded perspective.

- **Embrace small, mindful adjustments for lasting impact.** Small changes, like swapping caffeine for herbal tea or meditating before bed, can improve sleep and well-being. Consistent adjustments build a sustainable routine, helping you wake up refreshed and focused.

- **Develop a consistent sleep routine and calming bedtime ritual.** Establishing regular sleep and wake times, along with a calming bedtime routine, helps synchronise your body's rhythms. Simple rituals like reading or meditation support sleep-promoting hormones and bring balance to your day.

- **Optimise your sleep environment and manage screen time mindfully.** Create a peaceful sleep environment with blackout curtains, gentle lighting and minimal noise. Reduce screen time before bed, as blue light disrupts melatonin production, and instead opt for relaxing activities to ease into restful sleep.

- **Address stress mindfully and seek support when needed.** Managing stress with techniques like journaling or mindfulness reduces cortisol levels and supports deeper sleep. If sleep issues persist, seeking professional guidance can provide solutions that enhance your overall well-being.

Chapter 7
Breath in Balance:
Embracing Your Inner Rhythm

"Self-care is how you take your power back."
– Lalah Delia

Breathing is an act we often take for granted, an automatic flow that continues without a second thought. Yet, it profoundly affects our physical and mental well-being, especially in our professional lives. For working professionals – whether in an office, working from home, or managing a hybrid setup – the rhythm of your breath can become a powerful tool for managing stress, fostering resilience and staying connected to the present. In this chapter, we will delve into the transformative power of breath and how embracing mindful breathwork can help you relax, reduce stress and improve overall well-being.

By "embracing your breath," I mean learning to harness its natural rhythm to calm your nervous system, stay present and improve your daily life. Breathing serves as an anchor, a subtle yet powerful rhythm that has the potential to centre us amidst the constant demands of modern work life. In each breath lies the capacity to reset, restore and develop a state of calm, allowing us to navigate daily stressors with more resilience and clarity. As we explore the profound impact of mindful breathing, you will discover how something as simple as conscious breathwork can reshape your approach to work and well-being, providing a steady foundation for a balanced, fulfilling life.

The Physical and Mental Impact of Breathing

Our breath can feel restricted when hunched over a desk or slouched in a chair, often due to poor posture. This compressed posture restricts the diaphragm, making it difficult to take those deep, satisfying breaths that nourish us. Instead, we may default to shallow breathing, which limits oxygen intake, ramps up stress levels, and hinders our focus.

Research shows that engaging the diaphragm during breathing stimulates the vagus nerve,[1] an essential part of the autonomic nervous system, which helps calm the body and reduce stress. Small adjustments to our breathing patterns create a ripple effect, transforming mood, sharpening concentration and fostering a deeper sense of calm. In the modern workplace, stress builds up quickly, and our breath often mirrors this build-up by making it shallow and rapid.

This can happen particularly for remote professionals or those balancing work with home responsibilities, where makeshift set-ups – whether the couch or kitchen table – can challenge maintaining good posture. Slouching compresses the diaphragm, making deep, effective breaths harder to achieve. When breathing shifts to shallow chest breathing, the impact reaches beyond the physical. You may feel more fatigued, less focused or generally worn down. It is as though the body remains on high alert, reinforcing the mental load of a busy workday. Over time, this pattern can lead to a "new normal," where stress and tension build up, affecting both body and mind.

THE DIAPHRAGM FUNCTIONS IN BREATHING

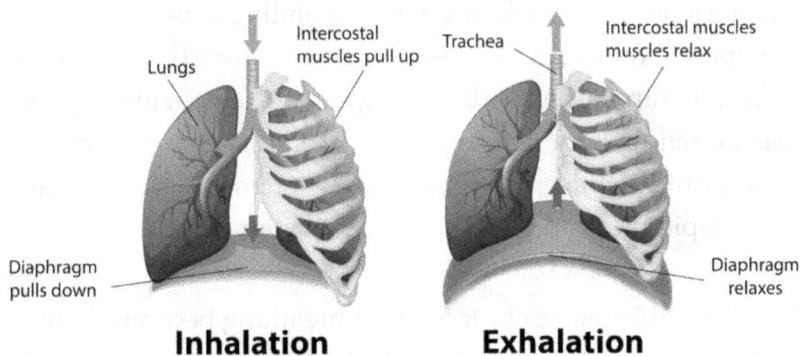

Intercostal muscles pull up

Lungs

Trachea

Intercostal muscles muscles relax

Diaphragm pulls down

Diaphragm relaxes

Inhalation

Exhalation

When we experience stress, our breathing patterns change immediately, becoming shallow, rapid and erratic. This shift is part of the body's natural response to perceived threats, activating the sympathetic nervous system to prepare for "fight or flight." In this state, the vagus nerve – the primary component of the parasympathetic system responsible for calming and restoring balance – is downregulated.

Consequently, stress hormones, particularly cortisol and adrenaline, flood the body, increasing heart, blood pressure and breathing rates. This shallow, chest-driven breathing often leads to physical symptoms like muscle tension, headaches, and breathlessness. Over time, this pattern can become ingrained, conditioning us to breathe more shallowly, even in non-stressful situations, which keeps the nervous system on high alert and inhibits the body's natural ability to relax and digest effectively.

For working professionals, the impact of stress on breathing can be especially apparent during high-pressure situations like tight deadlines, back-to-back meetings or juggling multiple projects. Imagine a professional focused on responding to urgent emails or preparing for a critical presentation. The stress of these tasks can lead to rapid, shallow breathing as they remain intently focused, often without realising they haven't taken a moment to pause or breathe deeply. Consider how often you notice shallow or rapid breathing while focused on your work tasks.

Over time, this tense, chest-focused breathing becomes habitual, sending constant signals to the body that it is in a state of alert. Physical symptoms – like shoulder tightness, headaches or that feeling of breathlessness – start to creep in, turning shallow breathing into an ingrained pattern.

Can you recall your experiences of physical symptoms like shoulder tightness, headaches or difficulty relaxing after work in your day-to-day life? This cycle doesn't just make it difficult for the body to relax after work; it interferes with digestion, sleep, and overall well-being as the body struggles to find balance.

In these situations, mindful breathing becomes a valuable tool for breaking the stress-breathing cycle. By consciously pausing for a few deep breaths, professionals can activate the vagus nerve, calm the nervous system and bring grounding and clarity into their day. I encourage you to take a moment and reflect on what might change in your workday if you took intentional pauses to breathe deeply, especially during high-stress moments.

The link between breath and digestion is essential, especially regarding mindful eating and preventing overeating. Shallow breathing signals the body to stay in heightened arousal when we eat while stressed, disrupting digestion. Stress diverts blood flow from the digestive organs, slowing metabolism and leading to indigestion or bloating. Moreover, hurried, shallow breaths while eating can inhibit the body's sense of fullness, increasing the likelihood of overeating.

Consciously breathing while eating, however, helps activate the vagus nerve, prompting a relaxation response that supports optimal digestion. By taking a few deep, slow breaths before and during meals, you can slow down, become more attuned to your body's hunger and fullness cues and enjoy the sensory experience of eating more fully. This practice of mindful breathing and conscious eating allows us to harness the breath to improve our relationship with food, reduce stress and foster a more holistic approach to nourishment.

This is where breathwork comes in as a simple yet powerful tool for managing stress and staying grounded. Breathwork refers to breathing techniques and mindful practices that regulate the body's responses to stress and overwhelm. In the context of polyvagal theory, conscious breathing directly impacts the vagus nerve,[2] helping to balance the nervous system and encouraging a sense of calm. This connects to mindfulness, where breath awareness is an anchor for staying present, and to the concept of play, where feeling relaxed and safe allows us to engage fully and joyfully.

The ability to influence your breath becomes a grounding resource, especially in the face of work pressures and the complex demands of remote and hybrid setups. When deadlines tighten, meetings multiply or the boundary between work and home blurs, it is easy to slip into the body's "fight, flight, or freeze" mode. Breathwork, however, allows you to create small moments of calm to reset and to re-centre. These small, mindful pauses support your mental resilience and bring clarity and focus, linking back to earlier chapters on polyvagal theory, mindfulness and sleep.

Reflecting on my own experience, I discovered the healing power of trauma-releasing breathwork during a particularly overwhelming period. Working with my breath coach, Nuri, I learned to reconnect with my body through guided, rhythmic breathing. This experience was transformative – allowing me to release deeply held tensions and confront emotions I hadn't realised were affecting me so profoundly. As I breathed, I began to understand how my emotional system, tuned to survival, shaped my perceptions of the world around me.

What is my reality? How do I see myself? These questions surfaced as I sat, breathing deeply and feeling the release of emotions from my past that were rooted deeply within me. With Nuri's guidance, I was able to observe and learn from these emotions in a space of safety and acceptance.

This journey revealed how much stress and unresolved trauma our bodies hold onto. Breathwork allowed me to shift from a hypervigilant state to one of calm and curiosity, ultimately helping me understand what it means to be truly present in my own body.

This process became an invaluable tool for managing the ups and downs of work and life, nurturing a deeper connection with myself, and fostering a sense of calm that I could carry with me. Breathwork isn't merely about managing stress; it is a way to reclaim your calm, one breath at a time.

The beauty of breathwork lies in its ability to activate the vagus nerve, helping you enter calming parasympathetic states that are essential for emotional regulation and well-being. I encourage you to explore breathwork with curiosity and compassion. Learning to harness your breath can be a gift you offer yourself daily, helping you ground yourself, manage stress and move forward with clarity.

As you explore the practices in this chapter, I encourage you to approach them with curiosity and patience. Breathwork is an invitation to tune in, find your centre and carve out moments of calm amidst the chaos that often surrounds us.

In my experience, allowing myself to slow down and embrace my breath was one of the simplest yet most profound gifts I could offer myself. It is a gentle reminder that amidst the chaos, we can always return to our breath – a powerful tool to support our well-being every day.

"When you arise in the morning, think of what a precious privilege it is to be alive, to breathe, to think, to enjoy, to love."
– Marcus Aurelius

Take a moment to notice how you breathe right now. Is your breath shallow or deep? Are you holding tension in your body? As you practise, remember that it is okay to take small steps. Every deep breath you take can lead you closer to a place of peace and clarity.

Embrace the journey with kindness towards yourself and recognise that you are not alone in this. We are all navigating life's challenges together, and sometimes, all it takes to shift our experience is a simple, conscious breath.

So, the next time you feel overwhelmed or distracted, pause and take a moment to breathe deeply. Let each breath be a reminder that you can shift your state, connect with your body and bring a sense of calm back into your day. Embrace the journey with patience and compassion, knowing every breath is a step towards greater well-being.

Practical Exercises: Cultivating a Breath-Centred Life

Breath is a powerful tool for reconnecting with ourselves, especially amidst life's busy pace. By observing and controlling our breath, we can tap into a wellspring of calm, clarity and resilience. This section will explore simple yet transformative breathing exercises rooted in polyvagal theory, mindfulness and a playful approach to life.

Whether navigating stress, seeking focus or simply wanting a few moments of peace, these exercises are designed to help you embrace breath as a resource for self-care and emotional balance.

If these practices are new to you, don't be discouraged; initially, it is natural for them to feel a bit unusual. The mind may try to distract you, offering instructions or opinions on how you "should" be doing it. With a bit of patience and practice, however, you will find that you can quiet these inner voices and allow your energy to settle into your breath.

Let us explore how these practices can bring more presence and ease into your daily experience.

Step 1: Awareness and Connection

First, start by becoming aware of your natural breath without altering it. Sit comfortably or lie on your back, close your eyes if it feels right, and allow yourself to simply observe. This is a mindful moment to connect with your body and anchor yourself in the present. Notice how your breath feels in your body, where it moves most freely, and where it feels more restricted.

Ask yourself the following questions:

1. How fast or slow is my breathing?

2. How deeply do I inhale and exhale?

3. Do I feel my ribs and abdomen move as I breathe?

4. Does my breath feel balanced, or is there a restriction on one side?

5. What does my breath sound like – soft, steady, laboured, shallow or resonant?

6. What signals is my nervous system sending me right now?

These questions help you tune into your body and understand how stress, posture or even a long day might influence your breathing. By observing without judgment, you are already creating a space for calm.

Step 2: The Slow Exhale Technique

When stress kicks in, our breath often becomes shallow and quick, feeding a cycle of tension. The slow exhale technique counters this by lengthening the exhalation, activating the parasympathetic nervous system and signalling safety to your body.

Try this: Take a deep, comfortable breath through your nose, feeling your belly expand. Then, slowly exhale through your mouth, engaging your abdominal muscles and ensuring the exhale is longer than the inhale. This allows the breath to be fully released from your stomach.

To further ground yourself in this experience, you can place one hand on your belly and the other on your chest, allowing you to feel the movement of your breath and the connection it creates within your body. Notice how this simple shift can quickly bring a sense of calm to your body and mind.

Tip: This technique is especially helpful during moments of pressure. Practice it before a meeting, during a break, or whenever you feel overwhelmed. It's a way to reset, even on a busy day.

Step 3: Box Breathing for Focus

Box breathing is a structured breathing technique that can be very grounding and centring, especially during high-stress moments. Start by inhaling for a count of four, holding the breath for four, exhaling for four, and then holding the empty breath for another count of four.

Repeat this cycle four to five times. Box breathing engages your mind with a simple counting rhythm, giving your body and nervous system a chance to reset.

Why it works: This practice balances the autonomic nervous system, easing anxiety and helping you to regain focus. Use it whenever you need to clear your mind and find balance – ideal for tight deadlines or before tackling a big project.

Step 4: Playful Breathing

Breathing can be fun! Add a bit of playfulness by trying variations like humming on the exhale, which gently vibrates the vagus nerve, or even practising gentle laughter as you exhale. Our voice is an embodied experience; engaging it through these practices deepens the connection between your breathing, body, and emotions. This invites lightness, stimulating the vagus nerve to promote relaxation and a sense of safety. Playful breathing techniques remind us that our breath can bring calm and joy, breaking up tension with moments of light-heartedness.

Incorporate play: Experiment with humming as you breathe out, or, if you feel like it, try a soft laughter exercise. These practices lift your mood and help you reconnect with a sense of safety and playfulness.

Step 5: Grounding Breath Breaks

Amidst the busyness of work, it can be easy to forget to breathe mindfully. Set reminders for short breath breaks throughout the day – just a minute or two is enough to create a small reset. During these breaks, breathe deeply, allowing yourself to pause. Notice any tension and reconnect with your body before continuing with your tasks.

Routine tip: Try integrating these grounding breath breaks into your schedule. They are a powerful reminder to check in with yourself, even during a busy day and a great way to help manage stress and keep a calm, focused mind.

These practical exercises offer a toolkit for returning to your breath and finding balance, even amid life's demands. By embracing these practices, you empower yourself with simple ways to reduce stress, strengthen focus, and bring a sense of presence into each day.

By embracing the transformative power of your breath, you are giving yourself a remarkable tool for managing the inevitable stresses of daily work life. Your breath offers a sensory experience that helps you reconnect with yourself, grounding you in the present moment. It allows you to reach a state where you can better tolerate and navigate the discomforts of daily stress while addressing your body's needs for rest and restoration.

This chapter explored how conscious breathing can engage the vagus nerve, calm the nervous system and develop a sense of balance – no matter where you are or what your day brings. The beauty of these practices is their simplicity; it is not about perfect posture or flawless breathing technique but about creating mindful moments to check in with yourself.

The takeaway here is simple but powerful: When you prioritise your breath, you gain the resilience to handle the ups and downs of life with greater ease.

These moments of awareness can serve as gentle reminders to connect with your body and mind, stepping back from the busyness to create a pocket of calm. Whether at a cluttered desk, working from a kitchen table, or even in a bustling café, a mindful breath offers a moment to reset. By prioritising your breath, you are nurturing physical well-being and encouraging emotional resilience and mental clarity.

These small, mindful pauses bring a sense of compassion into your routine, allowing you the grace to recharge and move forward with intention. So, the next time you feel overwhelmed, pause, take a few deep breaths and remember that this simple act can make all the difference in navigating your work life – and beyond.

Key Points

- **The power of breath in daily life.** Breath is a powerful anchor amidst the demands of modern work life, offering a steady foundation for calm, resilience and presence. Consciously tuning into your breath provides a simple yet transformative way to manage stress and improve well-being.

- **Impact of stress on breathing.** Stress causes shallow, rapid breathing, which signals the body to remain in a heightened state of alertness. Recognising this cycle empowers you to take mindful steps to break it, promoting a balanced, relaxed state.

- **Breath and the vagus nerve.** Engaging the diaphragm through intentional breathing stimulates the vagus nerve, activating the parasympathetic system responsible for calming the body and reducing stress. This is a natural pathway to resilience and emotional regulation.

- **Mindful breathing helps digestion.** Mindful breathing before and during meals helps the body shift out of stress mode, enhances digestion, and helps regulate appetite. This approach promotes a healthy relationship with food, encourages conscious eating, and prevents overeating.

- **Breathwork as a tool for emotional balance.** Conscious breathwork provides a toolkit for grounding and clarity, especially during high-pressure moments. Whether through slow exhales or playful breath exercises, these techniques help you reset, refocus and approach challenges calmly.

- **Empowerment through simple practices.** You develop a sense of self-compassion, resilience, and mental clarity by prioritising breath in small, mindful pauses throughout the day. These practices remind you to reconnect with your body and mind, bringing balance and presence into even the busiest days.

Chapter 8
Mindful Movement

"Force is the language of cells and movement is what we say."
– Dr Andreo Spina

Staying active in many traditional office settings can feel like an uphill battle. Limited facilities for exercise, tight schedules and a work culture that often prioritises deadlines over well-being make it challenging to prioritise movement. Desks and meeting rooms are designed with sitting in mind, and the hours can slip by without so much as a stretch. But here is the thing: There are ways to sneak movement into your day, even in environments that seem to work against it – from simple desk stretches to making the most of your lunch break. Small changes can add up, and we will explore these strategies throughout the chapter.

For those working from home, the flexibility of managing your own time is a gift that is easy to overlook. Without the daily commute or rigid office routines, you can integrate movement into your day in ways that feel good to you. It could be a quick stretch between meetings, a walk after lunch or setting up a little corner for yoga or a workout. This freedom to move whenever you want is one of the hidden gems of working remotely. However, the responsibility to move rests with you at home or in an office. Small, consistent efforts are what truly count. I have seen it with my clients – those little pockets of movement don't just help the body. They also uplift the mind. A few mindful stretches can melt away tension in your neck and back, a short walk can clear your head and a playful dance can shift your mood. Recognising that movement isn't just a chore but a necessity is important – one that nurtures our bodies, minds and spirits.

Let us connect this to the previous chapters on breathwork, polyvagal theory, mindfulness and sleep. Each element is vital to our overall well-being and is interconnected with movement. For instance, breath and movement go hand in hand. When we breathe deeply while stretching or exercising, we engage the diaphragm, stimulate the vagus nerve and activate our body's relaxation response. This synergy calms the nervous system and improves physical performance, making us more centred and present. Polyvagal theory emphasises the importance of feeling safe in our bodies so that when we incorporate movement, we can regulate our nervous system, moving from a state of fight-or-flight to one of safety and calm. Engaging in physical activity can signal to our bodies that we are thriving, reinforcing a sense of safety and connection to ourselves and our environment. Physical activity also plays an important role in supporting digestion, as movement stimulates the digestive system and helps maintain a healthy gut. Regular exercise, whether a brisk walk, yoga or more intense workouts, improves blood circulation, which aids the digestive organs in functioning optimally. Physical activity encourages peristalsis – the natural contractions of the intestines that help move food through the digestive tract. This gentle stimulation can be especially beneficial for people who experience sluggish digestion or bloating, as movement helps relieve these symptoms by promoting natural digestive flow.

Mindfulness, too, is woven into the fabric of movement. By practising mindfulness during physical activities – whether focusing on your breath while you stretch or being present as you walk – you develop a deeper awareness of your body and its needs.[1] This connection encourages self-compassion, allowing you to listen to what feels good and honour your body's signals. Lastly, let us not forget about sleep. The more we move, the better our bodies can rest. Regular physical activity contributes to better sleep quality, ensuring that we wake up refreshed and ready to tackle the day. Movement can help release pent-up energy and tension, paving the way for a more restful night's sleep.

So, as working professionals, finding ways to integrate movement into your day isn't just about staying fit – it is about nurturing your well-being. Start where you are, see what feels good and keep showing up for yourself, one movement at a time. By unifying breath, movement, mindfulness and the principles of polyvagal theory and understanding how they interconnect, you can create a holistic synergy that strengthens your body and nurtures the interconnected systems that keep you balanced and resilient. In this sense, movement becomes more than physical exercise – it is an essential practice that harmonises our digestion, tones the vagus nerve and creates a sense of well-being that ripples through every aspect of our lives.

Physical activity can sometimes seem like a distant goal in our often sedentary work lives – whether in traditional offices or working from home. Desk jobs and remote setups can make it easy to fall into a routine of prolonged sitting, which can have a ripple effect on our health. But bringing movement into our daily work routine is important for maintaining physical and mental well-being. Regular physical activity is a powerful antidote to the risks associated with a sedentary lifestyle. It helps prevent chronic illnesses like cardiovascular issues, diabetes and obesity. Apart from keeping fit, it also creates a buffer against the health risks of sitting too much.

Moreover, moving your body isn't just good for your heart – it is also fantastic for your mind. Physical activity stimulates the release of endorphins, those "feel-good" hormones that act as natural mood enhancers and painkillers.[2] Think of movement as a natural stress-buster. For office workers and remote employees alike, understanding how exercise boosts endorphin levels can help manage stress, boost mood and improve job satisfaction.

Beyond emotional benefits, regular movement supports cognitive functions such as memory, attention and executive function. A meta-analysis shows that physical activity improves cognitive performance, especially in older adults.[3] For those navigating complex projects or tight deadlines, better memory and focus from regular exercise can be a game-changer. Improved executive function from consistent movement helps with decision-making and organisation, which is essential for balancing workloads and achieving goals.

Office-Based Movements

Simple office-based movements can be a game-changer in addressing common issues like neck and shoulder tension, wrist strain and lower back discomfort. Practicing neck rolls, shoulder shrugs, wrist flexor and extensor stretches and mini workouts such as desk push-ups or chair squats can make a significant difference. Desk Yoga, including seated forward bends and spinal twists is another effective way to release tension and improve flexibility. Since working from home most of the time, a foam roller and trigger point balls have become my best friends – tools I often recommend to clients. Foam rolling is a type of self-myofascial release (SMR) and offers many benefits, such as pain relief, tension release, injury prevention and improved flexibility, mobility and circulation. The same goes for the trigger point ball. Both provide a focused and effective approach to self-care and can also be taken with you on work trips, vacations, to the office or when working from home.

If you don't have one, I'd encourage you to get either or both and play with them. You won't regret it!

Additionally, to support these efforts, consider using the array of apps available that offer reminders and guided exercises tailored for office workers. Whether it is desk yoga apps, stretch reminder apps or fitness trackers that prompt you to move throughout the day, technology can be a helpful ally. Organising group stretching or walking breaks with colleagues can also encourage a supportive and active work environment, making it easier to stay motivated. You could inspire and encourage your colleagues to keep active during the workday. So, go ahead. Take the lead!

If you are looking for personalised guidance, working with a personal trainer can be an excellent investment. A trainer can tailor workouts to fit your schedule and needs, help you stay accountable, correct any poor habits or posture and teach you new skills for independent training. Even a few sessions can offer invaluable support and boost your confidence in integrating movement into your routine. I understand that you might be concerned about the cost of these services, but think of it as an investment in yourself. It is a starting point for getting the support you need until you build the knowledge and autonomy to take charge of your own health. Joining a gym, possibly at a lower fee, can also offer access to group classes and facilities like saunas or steam rooms, which you might find beneficial. Every effort counts, no matter how small it may seem, and consistency is key.

To start integrating movement into your workday, take a moment to reflect on what exercise means to you personally. Think about the types of physical activity you enjoy, which you might not be so fond of, and envision movement fitting into your ideal day. Do you prefer taking short, frequent stretching breaks or longer, more focused exercise sessions at specific times? Understanding your preferences will help you create an enjoyable and sustainable routine. Once you understand what works for you, grab your planner and schedule regular movement breaks throughout your day. Set reminders to stand up, stretch or engage in quick physical activities that feel good. You can also outline a weekly physical activity plan with structured workouts and informal activities like walking or gardening. By making movement a regular part of your routine – not just something you try to fit in at the end of the day – you are setting yourself up for success. This approach keeps you on track and allows you to care for your body while balancing work demands, ensuring that physical activity becomes an integral, easy-to-maintain part of your day.

Practical Tips to Start

I encourage you to do this exercise now as you are more likely to set the intention and take action. Take time to think about your unique context and how you can make decisions that are realistic and sustainable:

1. **Reflect on your exercise preferences.** Ask yourself what types of movement and activities you enjoy or dislike. This might include activities like yoga, quick desk exercises, short walks or joining a group.

2. **Envision your ideal day.** Imagine how you would like to incorporate movement into your daily routine. Do you prefer morning stretches, lunchtime walks or afternoon workouts?

3. **Schedule breaks and activities.** Use a planner or a digital calendar to set alarms for regular breaks. Include stretches or brief physical activities to break up long periods of sitting.

4. **Plan your weekly activities.** Develop a weekly exercise schedule. Include formal workouts and informal activities

such as a brisk walk during lunch or a quick stretch every hour.

5. **Designate a movement space.** Creating a space for physical activity at home encourages regular movement.

6. **Take advantage of community resources.** Use local parks, gyms, or community fitness programs to support your physical activity goals.

7. **Consider hiring a personal trainer.** Personal training offers tailored guidance, accountability and motivation to help you achieve your fitness goals. It also provides a structured routine and pushes you through plateaus in your fitness journey.

Embodiment and Mind-Body Connection

Embodiment is the profound, integrative connection between mind and body that supports mental presence and emotional regulation. When we engage in regular movement practices, we strengthen this connection, becoming more attuned to our bodies and experiences. Research highlights the benefits of activities such as yoga, tai chi and mindful walking for improving body awareness and mindfulness.[4] These practices reduce stress and improve overall well-being by nurturing a state of presence and embodiment. For busy professionals, taking time to incorporate these activities into daily life can lead to a deeper understanding of oneself and a greater sense of calm amid the demands of work.

Yoga, for instance, combines physical postures, breathing exercises and meditation, all heightening body awareness and mindfulness. This ancient practice encourages an active focus on internal sensations, promoting greater self-awareness and emotional balance. Studies have shown that yoga is linked with neuroplasticity, aiding in developing new neural pathways that support learning and stress reduction.[5] Several of my clients, who hold high positions in their workplaces and have many responsibilities, have found that practising yoga significantly aids in their stress management. While they appreciate it for fitness reasons, they cherish it even more as a form of self-care, offering them the opportunity to calm, relax and reconnect with themselves.

Similarly, tai chi provides a unique approach to movement by emphasising slow, deliberate motions and deep breathing. It functions as a moving meditation, helping to centre the mind and body while encouraging relaxation and heightened bodily awareness.

Mindful walking is another valuable practice involving full attention to each step and bodily sensation. This simple yet profound way to stay grounded refines a deep connection with the present moment, making it an accessible option for busy professionals looking to integrate mindfulness into their day. During busy days, our senses can become overstimulated, leading to tiredness and, if not addressed, burnout. This overstimulation impacts the frequency at which our brains take in and emit signals. Walking through nature allows for healthy sensory stimulation, helping to shift the brain's frequency and endorse a more relaxed state of mind. Forest bathing, or *shinrin-yoku*, invites you to immerse yourself in nature's serenity. This practice, which originated in Japan, is more than just a walk in the woods – it is a mindful experience that allows you to absorb the calming energy of the forest. My Japanese friends introduced me to this technique long ago and the practice of walking barefoot on grass or the beach. If it is a rainy day and you cannot go outdoors, simply sitting in silence, allowing your senses to rest and recharge, can be equally restorative. During these mindful moments, be open to self-reflection and the tranquillity surrounding you. When stress or discomfort arises, closing your eyes, breathing deeply and embracing this peaceful environment can help shift your nervous system's response, aiding relaxation.

Healing Through Movement

Movement practices can also serve as powerful allies in trauma recovery. They create a supportive space where one can release tension, process emotions and ensure a sense of safety and empowerment within the body. Trauma often leaves a physical imprint, making movement-based therapies beneficial for addressing these somatic expressions. As we have discussed, everything is interconnected! Techniques such as somatic experiencing, developed by Peter Levine, focus on increasing awareness of bodily sensations to release stored trauma energy. This approach encourages individuals to become attuned to the physical manifestations of trauma – like muscle tension or shallow breathing – and uses gentle movements and grounding exercises to channel emotional and physical release.

Personally, I have been practising somatic techniques for years, and they have immensely supported my journey. I also use these techniques with my clients. Sometimes, it can be as simple as asking, "Where do you feel this emotion in your body?" When working with people, we pay close attention to their body language, as the body tells a story. However, just as much as we can observe what the body reveals, we must also question what it doesn't show. Often, the unspoken or unseen aspects hold as much significance, and by gently exploring these, we can create space for deeper healing and self-awareness.

Dance and movement therapy tap into expressive movement, allowing individuals to process emotions and trauma through spontaneous and creative movement. Both of these techniques support a deeper understanding of how trauma is stored in the body, facilitating a safe, gradual process of release and healing. For working professionals, acknowledging the impact of stress and trauma on the body is important. Several of my clients attend dance classes weekly, not just for fitness but for their mental health.

Most importantly, these classes are playful and fun, helping you manage stress, stay spontaneous and enjoy the activity without feeling pressured. This sense of playfulness and movement allows you to let go, reconnect with your bodies and take a break from the structured demands of daily life. By embracing this form of movement, you create space for both physical and emotional expression, making dance a valuable part of your overall self-care routine.

Self-Expression and Creativity

Movement is not solely about physical health. It is also a powerful form of self-expression and creativity. Engaging in movement allows you to communicate and process your inner experiences and emotions in ways that words sometimes cannot capture. Practices like improvisational dance encourage spontaneous movement, enabling you to express emotions freely without the constraints of structured choreography. This can offer a refreshing escape from the rigid routines of work and create a joyful outlet for creative expression. Expressive arts therapies, which combine movement with art, music and drama, provide holistic avenues for emotional expression and healing. Bringing these practices into your routine – whether through a quick dance break, a mindful walk or moments of creative exploration – can help you manage work pressures and reconnect with yourself. These activities alleviate stress and ignite creativity, introducing a touch of joy and playfulness into your day.

This sense of playfulness, closely tied to polyvagal theory, plays a vital role in regulating the nervous system. Engaging in spontaneous, joyful movement taps into the ventral vagal state, the part of the nervous system associated with feelings of safety, connection and social engagement. Inviting moments of play and creativity into your daily life activates this system, which helps reduce stress and supports emotional resilience. This playful approach to movement creates a state of presence and relaxation, making it a vital tool for well-being and productivity.

EXERCISE #1: Self-Expression

Physical Activity

Stand up and embody the sensation of lightness. Allow your body to express the feeling of moving effortlessly in the world, with the freedom to shape your own life and create new possibilities.

- Without words, how does your body communicate freedom, choice and endless possibilities?

- Reflect on your movements: Which parts of your body were most active? Describe the quality of their motion (e.g. unrestricted, somewhat limited. Give each style a name). Were there any repeating patterns? Were the movements expansive or contained, light or weighted?

- What insights did you gain about the way your body moves?

- What did you observe within your body?

- How do you feel now, having spent this time using your body as a means of expression?

EXERCISE #2: Body Language Awareness

Journal

Notice how your body communicates emotions. For example, does your posture shift with your mood? If you're feeling angry, do you still wear a smile? Are your gestures and facial expressions in sync with your inner feelings?

Give your body permission to tell the story of your emotion.

By embracing the mind-body connection through movement, you align physical activity with deeper emotional and mental expressions. This integration helps you stay grounded, improves your overall well-being and brings more direction into your daily life – whether navigating the demands of a busy office or enjoying the flexibility of working remotely. Movement is a powerful way to check in with yourself; it doesn't have to be complicated. Whether you find peace in a calming yoga session, joy in a lively dance break or relaxation in a mindful walk, remember that each movement you make is a step toward nurturing your body and mind.

These moments of movement are acts of self-care and empowerment. Every stretch, every breath, every playful moment of moving your body is an opportunity to reconnect with yourself, enhance your resilience and boost your energy for whatever the day throws at you. So, embrace these moments, no matter how small and let them be reminders that you care for your physical and emotional health. As you move through your day, remember that the more you nurture this connection, the stronger and more aware you will feel, ready to face the world with confidence, presence and a deep sense of well-being.

Key Points

- **The importance of daily movement.** Movement is a vital practice, not just for physical fitness but as an essential element of overall well-being. In traditional offices and home workspaces, integrating small, regular movements can break up sedentary patterns, relieve tension and elevate mood, helping you stay resilient and energised.

- **Synergy between movement and breathwork.** Deep breathing during movement engages the diaphragm and stimulates the vagus nerve, activating the body's relaxation response. This synergy between breath and movement calms the nervous system, improves physical performance and helps you feel more centred and present.

- **Movement for digestive health.** Physical activity supports digestion by promoting peristalsis, the natural movement of the digestive tract. This helps relieve bloating and sluggishness. Exercise also tones the vagus nerve, activating the "rest and digest" response and creating an optimal state for nutrient absorption and digestive health.

- **Mindfulness in movement.** Focusing on breath and body sensations during movement develops a deeper awareness of the body's needs. This mindful approach also develops self-compassion, allowing you to listen to and honour your body's signals. It strengthens the mind-body connection and improves emotional well-being.

- **Movement for mental clarity and cognitive performance.** Regular physical activity boosts endorphins, improves mood and enhances cognitive functions like memory and focus. This makes movement an invaluable resource for professionals, providing natural stress relief, sharper focus and improved executive function, which are essential for productivity and decision-making.

- **Self-expression and playful movement.** Movement is a powerful form of self-expression and creativity. Activities like dance, mindful walking or even spontaneous movement tap into the ventral vagal state, supporting feelings of safety, connection and emotional resilience. Embracing playful and joyful movement creates a balanced state of presence and relaxation, helping you reconnect with yourself in empowering ways.

Chapter 9
Holistic Kitchen

"Self-care is giving the world the best of you, instead of what's left of you."
– Katie Reed

Food is a fundamental part of our lives, shaping our physical health and emotional connections. Growing up in Croatia, I saw how meals were more than just food – they expressed love, hospitality and warmth. Meals were bonding moments, where conversations flowed and traditions were shared. However, in today's fast-paced world, many professionals are disconnected from this intimate relationship with food, opting for convenience over nourishment. How often do we hear ourselves or others say, "I don't have time to cook," or "I don't know where to start"? This struggle is all too familiar for busy professionals whose packed schedules make the idea of cooking feel daunting, leading us to choose quick, convenient options that often leave us feeling sluggish or unfulfilled.

This chapter will explore a holistic, mindful approach to food and nourishment. A holistic view means looking at food as more than just a source of calories or nutrients; it is a means of nurturing the body, mind and spirit. It involves recognising how our food choices influence our physical health, emotional well-being, energy and quality of life. Mindful eating, a cornerstone of this approach, is being fully present during meals – appreciating each bite and listening to our body's signals of hunger and fullness. It is about engaging in a nourishing experience that creates a deeper connection with ourselves. This holistic, mindful approach to nutrition is essential, especially for those managing busy schedules, working remotely, travelling or navigating hectic office routines. In such contexts, it is easy to fall into patterns of mindless eating, grabbing whatever is quick and accessible. Stress can also impact our choices, leading to habits like skipping meals, overeating or relying on processed foods, which can sap our energy, disrupt our mood and impair our sleep quality.

But rather than seeing healthy eating as something you *have to* do, what if you approached it as something you *get to* do? Here is where mindful goal setting comes in. Take a moment to ask yourself: *What does healthy nutrition mean to me?* Is it about having more energy during the day, feeling more balanced emotionally or improving your sleep quality? These questions matter because they help you connect your intentions with deeper values.

If being healthy, present and well-rested is important to you, how does the food you eat right now align with that? What would your life look like if you shifted towards more mindful, nourishing food choices? Imagine how much better you would feel if you had meals that fuelled you, not just physically but emotionally, too. Imagine feeling lighter, more energetic, more in tune with your body or sleeping more soundly at night.

Remote workers often face unique challenges that can impact their work and daily lives. Working from home might sound ideal – no commute, more flexibility and comfort. However, the reality can be more complex. Many remote workers struggle with blurred boundaries between work and personal life. Without the physical separation of an office, they often find it challenging to "switch off," which can lead to longer working hours, increased stress and burnout. This consequently leaves them feeling mentally drained and less inclined to cook healthy meals. This can result in relying on quick fixes like takeaways, processed snacks or skipping meals altogether. Over time, these choices can lead to poor nutrition, fluctuating energy levels and even weight gain, impacting overall health. Isolation is another common issue.

The feeling of isolation and loneliness can often drive people to turn to food for comfort, leading to emotional eating. Without the usual social interactions and colleague support, remote workers might find themselves reaching for snacks or indulging in comfort foods to fill that emotional gap. This coping mechanism can create an unhealthy cycle, where moments of loneliness or stress are temporarily soothed with food, often leading to weight gain, poor nutrition and feelings of guilt or sluggishness, which can further impact their mental and physical well-being.

Human connection is just so important and valuable, not solely for mental well-being but for feeling part of a team. When that is lacking, people may feel less engaged, which can impact their performance and job satisfaction over time. There is also the challenge of maintaining a healthy routine. Many remote workers report difficulties sticking to regular meal times, getting enough movement or even setting aside time for a proper lunch. It is easy to snack mindlessly, skip meals or rely on quick, often less nutritious options when you are just a few steps away from your kitchen but also always "on call." Over time, these habits can affect energy levels, mood and overall health. Another significant issue is ergonomics.

Home setups are rarely as well-designed as office spaces. Working from a sofa, bed or makeshift desk can lead to back, neck or shoulder pain, making work uncomfortable and disrupting sleep. Physical discomfort, compounded over weeks and months, can impact concentration and productivity, making even small tasks feel like a struggle.

All these factors create a cycle that impacts both work and personal life. Feeling isolated and burnt out at work often spills into personal life, affecting relationships, mood, nutrition and sleep quality. Just like mindful goal setting around physical health, remote workers can benefit from setting intentional goals around their nutrition and health. This process is about finding small ways to make the remote work experience more fulfilling and sustainable – taking breaks to move, eating meals mindfully, setting boundaries and reaching out for connection. By approaching remote work with a mindful, intentional perspective, it becomes not just something they "have to manage" but something they can shape to feel more energised, self-aware and empowered.

When I started focusing more on what I put into my body, I noticed a huge shift in how I felt. I had more energy during the day, my sleep improved and I felt clearer and more focused. I didn't have to overhaul everything at once – I just started with small, intentional changes that made a big difference over time. And that is the beauty of it. You don't need to be a gourmet chef or spend hours in the kitchen. Healthy eating doesn't have to be complicated. It is about making small, consistent choices that align with the bigger picture of how you want to live. When you start approaching food from a place of curiosity, asking questions like, "How will this nourish me? How will it make me feel?" becomes a much more meaningful and enjoyable part of your life.

Remember, food is not just about sustenance – it is a way to honour your body, connect with your values and nourish your physical, emotional and mental well-being. It certainly is not about perfection; it is about progress, and every small step you take toward more mindful eating brings you closer to a healthier, happier you.

The Nervous System's Role in Eating

The polyvagal theory, developed by Dr Stephen Porges, explains that our autonomic nervous system has three main branches: the sympathetic (fight or flight), the dorsal vagal (shutdown or freeze) and the ventral vagal (social engagement and connection) pathways.[1] When stressed, our body prioritises survival, diverting energy from digestion and other non-essential functions. This stress-induced state can lead to poor food choices, often high in sugar and fat – foods that provide quick energy but lack the nutrients necessary for long-term health. Stress also disrupts the balance of hormones like cortisol, increasing cravings for high-energy, comforting foods. These foods activate the brain's reward centre, releasing dopamine – a neurotransmitter associated with pleasure – but this temporary relief can often lead to overconsumption and feelings of guilt or discomfort afterwards. This temporary relief from stress through high-sugar or high-fat foods can sometimes lead to a cycle resembling addiction. When we frequently turn to these foods for comfort, we reinforce a pattern in the brain's reward system, making it harder to break away from these cravings over time. Recognising this pattern with compassion allows us to gently shift towards more mindful choices, finding healthier ways to soothe and support ourselves without relying on food as an emotional crutch.

Take a moment to reflect: Can you recall when you were stressed and noticed how it impacted your food choices? Were you craving sweets, deep-fried foods or complex carbs? Maybe you were overeating or even eating late at night when your body needed rest instead. I know I have been there. During particularly stressful times, I used to reach for sugar – ice cream especially – because it gave me a quick hit of energy and comfort. But after the rush, I always felt more drained and unfocused, leaving me to deal with both the emotional weight of stress and the physical discomfort of poor food choices such as swollen joints. This is where mindful eating can be transformative.

Research shows that mindful eating practices can help regulate our stress response, reducing cortisol levels and allowing the body to shift into the parasympathetic state, which supports better digestion and a sense of calm.[2] When we eat mindfully, we are more present with our food and more in tune with our body's natural hunger and fullness cues. This helps us make nourishing food choices that satisfy us in a more meaningful way without the emotional overeating that often comes from stress.

So, the next time you feel overwhelmed, pause for a moment instead of reaching for the nearest sugary or salty snack. Check in with yourself. Ask, "What does my body really need right now?" Perhaps it is not food that you truly need. Maybe your body is craving love and warmth, a sense of compassion or simply the feeling of being understood and listened to. Sometimes, what we seek in food is actually a longing for connection or comfort. It could be that you need a moment of stillness, a deep breath or even just a hug to soothe that inner tension.

When we slow down and listen to what our body is really asking for, we may realise that nourishment comes in many forms, and it is not always about what is on our plate. You might find that instead of a quick-fix snack, what you really need is a walk outside, a chat with a friend or some gentle self-care.

By taking this mindful approach, you will feel more grounded and connected to your body's needs, making it easier to avoid automatic cravings that don't truly serve your long-term health and well-being.

The Gut-Brain Connection and Mental Health

The gut-brain connection is a burgeoning field of study. The gut contains around 100 million neurons and produces about 90% of the body's serotonin, a neurotransmitter that regulates mood, sleep and cognitive function. Recent research shows that a healthy gut microbiome – composed of beneficial bacteria – plays a crucial role in mental health by influencing the production of neurotransmitters and reducing inflammation in the body.

Numerous studies emphasised the importance of the gut microbiota in mental health. For instance, it has been found that an imbalanced gut, or gut dysbiosis, is linked to conditions such as anxiety, depression and cognitive decline.[3] Poor diet, stress and lack of sleep all contribute to an unhealthy gut, but a diet rich in prebiotics (fibre-rich foods like whole grains, fruits and vegetables) and probiotics (fermented foods like yoghurt, kimchi and sauerkraut) can restore this balance and promote mental well-being.

Processed foods, on the other hand, tend to be low in nutrients and high in sugars, refined carbs and unhealthy fats. These foods can disrupt the delicate balance of our gut bacteria, lowering serotonin production and triggering inflammation. You might have noticed that you feel sluggish, irritable or even anxious after a meal filled with processed or fast food. This isn't just in your mind – there is a biological reason for it. Without the essential nutrients that promote healthy gut bacteria, your body struggles to produce the serotonin needed to keep your mood balanced, your mind sharp and your sleep restful.

Think about it: Have you ever reached for that quick snack or frozen meal after a busy day, only to feel more stressed or restless? It is not just the food – it is how that food affects your gut and, ultimately, your brain. By choosing more nourishing options, like adding whole grains, fresh fruits, vegetables and fermented foods into your diet, you are feeding your body and supporting your mental health.

This ties directly into the other key areas we've discussed, like movement, sleep, play, mindfulness and polyvagal theory. Movement, for instance, stimulates gut motility and helps keep our digestive system functioning well by stimulating regular muscle contractions in the intestines, which aids in the smooth movement of food through the digestive tract. Regular physical activity benefits not only your muscles and joints but also your gut bacteria. Incorporating mindful movement practices like yoga or even a simple walk can aid digestion, reduce inflammation and promote serotonin production, helping to reinforce the gut-brain connection. Sleep, too, is deeply intertwined with gut health.

When your gut is balanced, you are more likely to enjoy restorative, uninterrupted sleep. This is because a healthy gut microbiome supports serotonin and melatonin production – key hormones that regulate your sleep-wake cycle. If your diet is poor, leading to gut dysbiosis, it can cause sleep disruptions, further impairing your mental clarity and mood. When we talk about optimising your sleep, the nourishment your gut receives is important.

Let us also not forget about play and how it links to our nervous system's ability to regulate stress. As we explored in previous chapters, play activates the social engagement system within the polyvagal theory, bringing us into that safe, connected parasympathetic state where optimal digestion and nutrient absorption happen. Engaging in play activates our parasympathetic nervous system, allowing the body to relax and digest more effectively. This relaxed state encourages us to approach food with curiosity and enjoyment – trying new recipes, experimenting with ingredients and even savouring the process of preparing our meals. This playful, relaxed attitude towards food can improve digestion, as we are more likely to eat mindfully, chew thoroughly and genuinely appreciate each meal, all of which support optimal digestion and nutrient absorption.

The same goes for mindfulness. When we are mindful of our food choices and slow down to enjoy and savour our meals, we are engaging our senses and supporting our nervous system to stay in that relaxed, "rest and digest" mode, as polyvagal theory describes. Mindful eating, like mindful movement and mindful sleep practices, can help shift us from the fight-or-flight mode into a calmer, more grounded state where our body can focus on repair, digestion and healing.[4] In addition, oxytocin, often referred to as the bonding hormone, is released during social interactions and in response to food intake.[5] This hormone, triggered by sensory stimulation through actions like eating or physical closeness, plays a crucial role in everyday well-being and stress management. While oxytocin can enhance relaxation and reduce anxiety, there is a risk that people may rely on food or other behaviours like sex as a coping mechanism when relationships are strained, or anxiety levels are high. Ultimately, food is not just fuel; it's a complex chemical and biological process in the body that triggers a cascade of reactions, influencing our emotions, stress levels and overall well-being. Each small, mindful choice you make – moving your body, improving your sleep, playing or nourishing yourself with whole foods – strengthens that healthy connection between body, mind and soul.

Cognitive Health: Foods to Nourish Your Brain

What we eat plays a critical role in how our brain functions. In recent years, research has continued to uncover how certain foods can enhance cognitive health, protect the brain and improve focus. For example, a 2019 study found that diets high in refined sugars are directly linked to poorer cognitive outcomes.[6] The inflammatory response triggered by these sugars disrupts memory and learning, which can have long-term effects on brain health. Similarly, trans fats – commonly found in processed and fried foods – have been shown to damage brain cells and contribute to cognitive decline. Additionally, a study confirms that these fats not only affect brain signalling but also increase the risk of neurodegenerative illnesses like Alzheimer's.[7] For working professionals, especially those working remotely, cognitive health is essential for maintaining focus, productivity and mental clarity throughout the day.

HEALTHY EATING TIPS

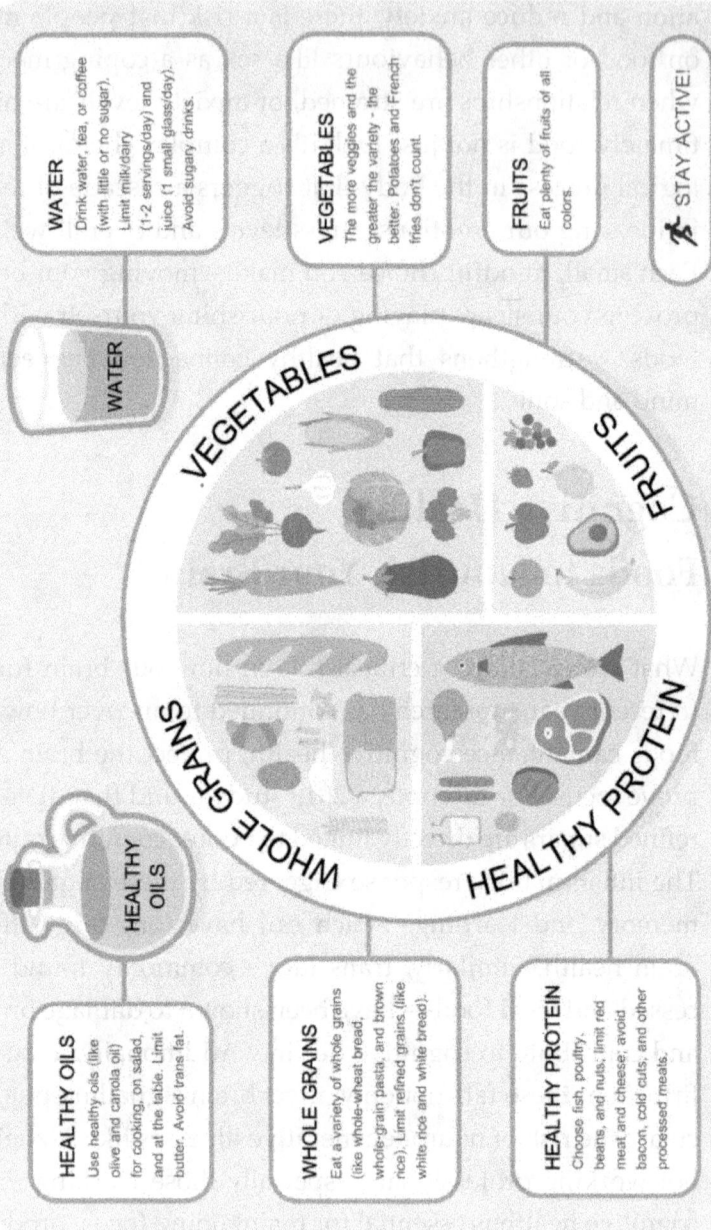

WATER
Drink water, tea, or coffee (with little or no sugar). Limit milk/dairy (1-2 servings/day) and juice (1 small glass/day). Avoid sugary drinks.

VEGETABLES
The more veggies and the greater the variety - the better. Potatoes and French fries don't count.

FRUITS
Eat plenty of fruits of all colors.

🏃 STAY ACTIVE!

WATER

VEGETABLES

FRUITS

WHOLE GRAINS

HEALTHY PROTEIN

HEALTHY OILS

HEALTHY OILS
Use healthy oils (like olive and canola oil) for cooking, on salad, and at the table. Limit butter. Avoid trans fat.

WHOLE GRAINS
Eat a variety of whole grains (like whole-wheat bread, whole-grain pasta, and brown rice). Limit refined grains (like white rice and white bread).

HEALTHY PROTEIN
Choose fish, poultry, beans, and nuts; limit red meat and cheese; avoid bacon, cold cuts, and other processed meats.

On the other hand, certain foods can be incredibly nourishing for the brain. Berries, rich in antioxidants and flavonoids, offer protective benefits against oxidative stress and inflammation linked to cognitive ageing. With their high content of ALA, a type of omega-3 fatty acid, walnuts have been shown to improve memory and cognitive function.[8] Additionally, whole grains such as quinoa and oats provide the brain with a steady source of glucose, helping to improve focus and reduce mental fatigue while supporting gut health, which further impacts cognitive performance. By prioritising foods that enhance brain health, remote workers can better handle the demands of their work, sustain focus and improve resilience to daily stressors.

A Client's Transformative Experience

A client of mine, William, has experienced firsthand how changing his relationship with food improved his physical health and mental clarity. As a frequent international traveller for work, William struggled with maintaining a consistent exercise routine, sleep schedule and balanced nutrition. With different time zones, constant travel and eating out regularly, he found it hard to stick to healthy habits. Despite being mindful of his diet, the restaurant meals often left him feeling bloated and fatigued due to the high levels of oil, salt and sugar.

Seeking a deeper understanding of how food affected his body, William began using Zoe, a blood sugar sensor, to track how he responded to different meals. This gave him incredible insight into how specific foods impacted his energy levels and overall health. With this knowledge, he started cooking more at home, and rather than seeing this as a chore, he embraced the process with curiosity and creativity. He began experimenting with new recipes and trying different ingredients that better aligned with his health goals. I love checking in with William to see what new dish or food he has discovered – what began as a way to manage his health has turned into a joyful exploration of flavours, playfulness and creativity in the kitchen.

William's journey is an excellent reminder that mindful changes can have a profound effect even with a hectic lifestyle. Small steps like cooking at home or selecting nutrient-dense foods over processed options can significantly improve physical health and mental well-being. His story shows that when we shift our perspective on food – seeing it not just as fuel but as nourishment and a source of connection – we can find joy in eating and preparing meals.

Steps to Achieve a Mindful and Holistic Approach to Nourishment

In today's fast-paced world, it is easy to lose touch with our body's signals about hunger and fullness. For many professionals, especially those working from home or constantly moving, meals can feel like just another task to rush through. But by taking a more mindful and holistic approach to nourishment, we can transform how we experience food – from something that simply fills us up to something that truly nourishes both body and mind.

These small, intentional steps can help you reconnect with your body and balance your eating habits. When you approach food with mindfulness, it transforms from fuel to a self-care practice and an opportunity to feel grounded, connected and nourished.

Here are some practical ways to do just that:

1. **Tune in to your body's signals.** Before you eat, take a moment to check in with yourself. Are you hungry or reaching for food out of habit, boredom or stress? It is so easy to grab something to eat without realising whether we need it or not. This simple act of tuning in can be incredibly grounding, helping you make food choices that better serve your needs. I often do this myself – if I reach for a snack, I'll pause and ask, "Am I actually hungry?" The answer surprises me more often than not.

   Remember the chapter on polyvagal theory and mindfulness? Checking in with your nervous system can provide valuable insights into your body's needs. When we tune in, we engage our parasympathetic nervous system, creating a sense of safety and connection that allows us to understand our cravings and emotions better. This mindful awareness creates a deeper relationship with food, transforming eating from a mere habit into an intentional act of nourishment. By recognising our body's signals, we empower ourselves to make choices that align with our values.

2. **Create a calm eating environment.** Wherever possible, try to sit down and minimise distractions during meals. Eating while working at your desk or scrolling on your phone is tempting, but this habit can disconnect you from the experience of eating. Engaging in these distractions often acts

as avoidance behaviour, keeping us in heightened alertness linked to our fight or flight system. Although we might think we are relaxing by multitasking, we inadvertently add more stress because we aren't fully present in the moment.

Even when time is limited, taking a brief moment of calm before your meal signals to your body that it is time to relax and digest. Whether at home, in the office or on the go, making mealtime a mindful practice can significantly improve how you feel afterwards. By consciously stepping away from distractions, you allow yourself to savour the experience of nourishing your body, creating a deeper connection to your food and embracing your overall well-being.

3. **Slow down and savour your meal**. Eating slowly allows your body to catch up with your mind. By giving yourself the time to savour each bite, you are more likely to recognise when you are full and satisfied. This practice embodies mindfulness, as it encourages you to be present with every mouthful, noticing the textures, flavours and overall enjoyment of the experience. When we eat slowly, we engage our sensory receptors, allowing our nervous system to process this information effectively.

This engagement activates the ventral vagal system, which promotes feelings of safety and connection. In contrast, eating quickly – often without thoroughly chewing – can stimulate the sympathetic nervous system, triggering our fight or flight response. This can lead to feelings of stress and discomfort, making it harder to tune into our body's signals.

This intentional eating approach improves our physical experience and encourages a deeper sense of mindfulness and presence in our daily lives.

4. **Balance your plate.** Aim to include a variety of foods that support your body's needs – carbohydrates, healthy fats, protein and plenty of fruits and vegetables. Each meal is an opportunity to nourish your body, and a balanced plate ensures you're getting the range of nutrients needed to thrive. This approach also makes meals more enjoyable and leaves you feeling mentally and physically satisfied.

   However, you don't necessarily have to stick to three traditional large meals daily. Smaller, balanced meals spaced throughout the day can be more manageable for many people, especially if you feel sluggish or hungry between meals. By breaking meals down into smaller portions, you can maintain steady energy levels, keep your metabolism active and prevent overeating. This also allows you to be more mindful of how your body feels throughout the day, adjusting your food intake based on your hunger and energy needs. This flexibility in how we nourish ourselves helps to remove the pressure and makes the experience of eating more intuitive and enjoyable.

5. **Stay hydrated.** Often, what feels like hunger can actually be thirst. Drinking water throughout the day helps maintain energy levels and supports digestion. You might find that staying hydrated keeps you feeling more vibrant and improves your focus and clarity throughout the day. Have you

ever noticed a dip in your energy, only to realise that you simply needed a glass of water?

It is essential to remember that dehydration can have significant effects on cognitive function. Studies show that even mild dehydration is linked to headaches, fatigue and brain fog, making concentrating or thinking clearly challenging.[9] In our fast-paced lives, it is easy to overlook the basic act of drinking enough water. By prioritising hydration, you nourish your body and optimise your brain health, ensuring that you stay sharp and alert throughout the day. So, the next time you feel a bit off, consider reaching for a glass of water before any snacks; it is the refreshing boost you need!

By making these mindful choices, nourishment becomes more than just something we do; it becomes a way to honour and care for our bodies, supporting our physical and emotional well-being.

Mindful eating is a form of self-care. It is about what you eat as well as how you eat. By slowing down, paying attention to your senses and immersing yourself in the present moment, you can transform food into a powerful tool for healing. Before meals, consider taking a few deep, mindful breaths.

This simple yet effective practice stimulates the vagus nerve, encouraging parasympathetic activation and helping your body shift into "rest and digest" mode. Studies show that engaging in mindful breathing before meals can improve digestion and nutrient absorption, setting a positive tone for your meal.[10]In our busy lives, it is all too common to push through exhaustion, relying on convenience foods to fuel our days. However, this approach only perpetuates a cycle of fatigue and poor nutrition. Embracing small, intentional changes – such as cooking fresh meals, eating mindfully and incorporating light movement – can significantly improve your overall well-being.

Try to avoid heavy meals, caffeine and alcohol before bedtime, as these can disrupt your sleep quality. Instead, opt for lighter, balanced snacks in the evening to support digestion without causing discomfort, such as a handful of nuts or a small piece of fruit. Staying hydrated throughout the day is important, but remember to limit fluid intake before bed to help prevent those disruptive late-night bathroom trips.

Reclaiming your relationship with food involves reconnecting with your true needs – listening to the signals your body sends, slowing down and being mindful of how you nourish yourself. Food isn't just about fuel; it is a means to support your mental clarity, physical health and emotional well-being. When you approach eating with intention and care, you will likely discover a newfound appreciation for the flavours and textures of your meals, turning each bite into an opportunity for joy and nourishment.

As you journey toward mindful eating, remember that it is not about perfection but progress. Mindfulness in our food choices helps us stay connected to our bodies, soothes the nervous system and encourages a balanced state that supports healthier, more intentional decisions aligned with our overall well-being and long-term goals. Celebrate each step you take, and allow yourself the grace to learn and grow along the way. Your relationship with food can evolve into a source of strength, empowerment and healing—one meal at a time.

Key Points

- **Holistic, mindful approach to food.** A holistic view of nutrition sees food as more than fuel; it nurtures the body, mind and spirit. This approach encourages mindful eating, where each bite is savoured, helping you reconnect with your physical and emotional needs for a healthier, more fulfilling relationship with food.

- **Impact of work-life balance on nutrition for remote workers.** Remote workers often face blurred boundaries between work and home life, leading to longer hours and reliance on quick, processed meals. Setting intentional nutrition goals can help you break unhealthy cycles, improving your energy levels and overall health.

- **Polyvagal theory and stress-related eating.** The polyvagal theory explains how stress shifts us into a "fight or flight" state, impacting digestion and food choices. Recognising this pattern and using mindful eating techniques helps shift the body into a calm, "rest and digest" mode, promoting healthier, more nourishing choices.

- **Gut-brain connection and cognitive health.** A healthy gut microbiome supports serotonin production, which affects mood, sleep and cognitive function. Choosing foods rich in probiotics and prebiotics boosts gut health and enhances mental clarity, emotional stability and resilience.

- **Mindful eating as self-care.** Mindful eating is more than just focusing on nutrients; it is a form of self-care that honours the body's needs. By slowing down and tuning in, you can transform meals into nourishing experiences that develop emotional balance and self-connection.

- **Empowering small changes in daily habits.** Small, consistent choices, such as staying hydrated, eating balanced meals and embracing light movement, can profoundly impact well-being. These intentional changes improve mental clarity, physical health and emotional stability, empowering you to improve your daily lives.

Chapter 10
Radiant Arrival: Embracing Your Workday With Confidence and Presence

"Talk to yourself like someone you love."
– Brené Brown

How we approach our mornings can set the tone for everything that follows. For many professionals – especially those working remotely or from home – a consistent morning routine is transformative in managing stress, maintaining focus and boosting productivity. A mindful, intentional start prepares you for the day's challenges, easing any rushed or scattered feelings that might otherwise lead to heightened stress and reduced productivity. A well-structured morning routine provides a sense of calm and focus, much like the foundation of a solid building, giving you a strong start. Think of your morning routine as the groundwork for a balanced day. Simple yet impactful practices such as five minutes of deep breathing, gentle stretching or a moment of gratitude can reset your nervous system, inducing calm and clarity. These grounding techniques activate your ventral vagus nerve, which supports a sense of safety and connection. Starting your day this way makes you more resilient and equipped to manage unexpected stressors and navigate your work with greater presence and purpose.

For example, starting the day with grounding breathwork can help you stay centred if an important meeting is scheduled. This physiological shift calms pre-meeting nerves, particularly in high-stakes situations where you might feel pressure to perform. Taking a few minutes to visualise yourself handling the meeting with calm confidence can reinforce your ability to show up authentically, actively listening and responding thoughtfully to those around you. Similarly, if you are preparing for a challenging presentation, beginning your day with gentle stretches can ease physical tension, helping you feel both grounded and energised. Following this with focused breathwork can improve clarity, calm performance anxiety and prepare you to speak confidently. Before stepping into the presentation, taking another brief moment to reconnect with your breath can re-establish the calm, focused state you cultivated in the morning, allowing you to present with poise and clarity. These small practices make a noticeable difference, helping your message resonate more effectively.

This approach to a morning routine isn't just for starting the day – it is a toolkit for navigating challenges, meetings and any interactions that require clarity and calm. Incorporating these techniques before critical conversations or high-stakes tasks creates an emotional buffer that allows you to engage fully and authentically, enabling you to confidently show up in every interaction.

Reflect on how your morning practices align with your core values. Embracing authenticity and maintaining a positive outlook can shape your day and the days of those around you. When you take time to develop calm and positivity, you set a ripple effect into motion. As polyvagal theory suggests, feeling safe and connected activates our social engagement system, enhancing our ability to relate to others. Beginning your day with intention and positivity enables your energy to resonate with others, creating a supportive, collaborative environment. Difficult conversations can also benefit from this mindful start. Grounding practices, like a few moments of gratitude, encourage a receptive mindset. Visualise the conversation going smoothly and set an intention to approach it calmly, perhaps as a patient listener or a composed communicator. This intentional shift can ease the stress of high-stakes interactions and help you respond rather than react. Grounding yourself with breathwork helps you maintain your centre, no matter how challenging the interaction may feel. Creating this mental and emotional buffer in the morning allows you to approach the conversation with greater compassion and openness.

Your morning routine, in essence, becomes a powerful tool for building resilience and setting a balanced, centred tone for your day. Whether a few minutes of breathwork, gentle stretching or mindful reflection, a consistent routine builds a positive foundation, helping you move through the day with greater ease, focus and purpose. By understanding how these practices work in harmony with your nervous system, you nurture your well-being while contributing to healthier workplace culture – whether in a shared office or working from home. During these practices, it is natural for uncomfortable emotions and thoughts to emerge. Feelings of self-doubt, frustration or even self-criticism arise as the mind is conditioned to react and judge. This is a common experience – especially when we give ourselves space to pause. Rather than resisting or trying to suppress these thoughts, gently acknowledge them and let them pass. Imagine these thoughts like clouds drifting across a sky, present but temporary. As you continue connecting to your heart, breath and intention, this practice becomes easier and more familiar. Each time you breathe deeply and ground yourself, you strengthen your ability to face discomfort with compassion and resilience. Over time, this intentional practice builds your brain's flexibility and enhances neuroplasticity – the brain's remarkable ability to rewire itself and form new connections. By repeatedly guiding your mind away from reactive thoughts and towards a state of calm and clarity, you are training your brain to respond with greater ease and balance in challenging situations. Creating calm brings immediate benefits while gradually rewiring your brain, creating a stronger foundation for resilience, adaptability and emotional well-being in the long run.

Adding grounding practices to your morning routine also helps you connect more meaningfully with others. Starting your day with a calm, centred mindset makes it easier to tackle challenges with ease and confidence. This balanced approach helps you fully engage with your work, handle professional demands with grace and create a more positive, productive experience for yourself and those around you.

By building this awareness and resilience in the morning – or at any time during the day, for that matter – you are setting yourself up to respond thoughtfully rather than react impulsively.

This mindful start creates a ripple effect, positively impacting your relationships, work environment and overall well-being. Every day becomes a fresh opportunity to grow, connect and contribute to a healthier, more balanced workplace.

How to Create a Calm and Centred Start

You don't need to practise all of these techniques at once. Start with the ones that resonate with you the most, those you feel naturally drawn to. Give yourself permission to play with them, experiment and tune into how each makes you feel. As you progress, you can gradually introduce other practices, noticing how your body and mind respond. This is your opportunity to personalise your routine into something uniquely yours. Consider journaling your thoughts, capturing any shifts or insights along the way. You might even create a vision board or sketch how you envision your journey, adding a creative, expressive layer to your practice. Remember, this is an evolving process – act, observe, adjust and refine as you go, allowing your routine to grow with you and reflect your inner world.

Here are some steps to help you develop a radiant arrival each morning and prepare for important meetings.

Step 1: Wake Up Mindfully

Before reaching for your phone or diving headfirst into emails, take a moment to breathe. A few deep breaths can do wonders, resetting your nervous system and inviting calm into your day. Feel your breath enter and exit your body, grounding you in the present moment. This simple act endorses clarity and focus, setting a peaceful tone for the day ahead.

While in this space, take a moment to observe any areas of tension within your body. Bring your awareness gently to these spots, breathing into them with intention and inviting relaxation to flow through. As you do, release any lingering tension or negativity, allowing your body to soften and settle into a state of calm. This is also a perfect moment to set intentions for your day – either in your mind or in your journal or even placing them on your vision board. You can reflect on what you are grateful for, visualise a successful workday and empower yourself with positive energy. So, even before you rise from your bed, you will have already centred yourself, set your tone and empowered yourself to start your day with purpose and confidence.

Step 2: Move Your Body

Engaging in gentle movement first thing can boost circulation and energise your spirit. Whether you stretch, do some yoga or take a brisk walk, movement connects you to your body and the present moment. Notice how moving awakens your senses, making you more receptive to the day's opportunities. Remember, this isn't and shouldn't be a strenuous workout. It is about being kind to yourself and allowing your body to shake off the remnants of sleep.

As you move, incorporate your breath to centre yourself. With each inhale, ground your body and, with each exhale, feel any tension release. In this space of mindful movement, you can also empower yourself with positive intentions for the day. Take a moment to express gratitude, perhaps saying, *"I am grateful for my body's strength and all it provides me with each day."* Feel that strength rise within you as you move with intention and ease, noticing each muscle as it awakens. This practice nurtures your body and mind, setting a foundation of confidence and gratitude as you start your day.

Step 3: Set Intentions for Your Day

What do you want to achieve today? How do you want to manifest your intentions at work? Setting intentions aligns your actions with your goals and values, boosting productivity and emotional well-being. Consider writing down your intentions or stating them aloud. This practice deepens your sense of agency and empowers you to make choices that reflect your authentic self.

Starting your workday with clear intentions is a powerful practice that helps you stay focused and aligned with your goals. Rather than diving straight into tasks, pause to create space for reflection. Ask yourself: *What do I want to achieve? How do I want to interact with others?* Setting intentions boosts productivity and influences how you carry yourself throughout the day. Like with mindful movement or nutrition planning, setting intentions honours yourself, creating a sense of purpose and direction. When combined with mindfulness, your focus and clarity increase, allowing you to easily navigate your workday.

Step 4: Embrace Your Authenticity

One of the most empowering things you can do as a professional is to bring your authentic self to your work. Authenticity means staying true to who you are – your values, beliefs and personality – rather than conforming to roles or expectations that don't reflect your true self. Authenticity can be a game-changer in a world where it is easy to slip into personas that don't align with who we are. When you allow yourself to show up genuinely, you build more meaningful connections with colleagues and clients, creating a sense of trust and openness.

Authenticity also aligns with polyvagal theory, which teaches that safety and connection are vital for our nervous system to function optimally. Being true to yourself can trigger the social engagement system, making your workday smoother and more enjoyable.

Take a moment to reflect on your authenticity:

- How can I bring more of my true self into my work today?

- What values do I want to honour in my interactions?

- Where have I been holding back, and how can I show up more fully?

By checking in with yourself, you can create deeper connections and a more fulfilling work experience.

Step 5: Release Negativity

Negative thoughts and emotions can weigh you down, limiting your potential and draining your energy before the day even begins. Acknowledging these feelings without allowing them to control your mindset is important. By releasing negativity, you create space for clearer thinking and better decision-making. As discussed in the chapter on breathwork, taking a few moments to breathe deeply can reset your nervous system and release the tension that clings to negative thoughts.

Remember, your body holds onto stress and trauma in ways you might not always realise. Releasing negativity is not just a mental task but also a physical one. This is where mindful movement can be incredibly effective. Whether it is stretching, foam rolling or simply taking a few mindful breaths, these actions can help shift that energy.

Take a moment to check in with your nervous system. Listen to what it is telling you. Befriend your nervous system and create an environment where your body feels safe and supported. Our bodies respond to our environment, so be open to the reciprocity your surroundings allow.

As you do this, consider these reflection prompts:

- What sensations is my body experiencing right now?

- Where am I holding tension, and what can I do to release it?

- How can I create an environment that promotes calm and safety for my nervous system?

- What does my body need to feel grounded and supported today?

This invites a gentle and holistic approach to release negativity while building awareness of the body's signals.

Step 6: Practice Gratitude

Gratitude is an incredibly effective way to shift your mindset towards positivity and abundance. Before you start your workday, take a moment to reflect on what you are grateful for – whether it is the opportunities ahead, the resources you have or even the lessons learned from past challenges. Gratitude connects to the body in profound ways, impacting your emotional state and your nervous system. By nurturing a sense of appreciation, you activate the parasympathetic nervous system, helping to reduce stress and encourage a sense of calm. It is a small practice with big benefits that ties into our earlier discussions on mindful movement, breath and sleep. Gratitude creates a foundation of peace, which helps you navigate the pressures of work with greater resilience.

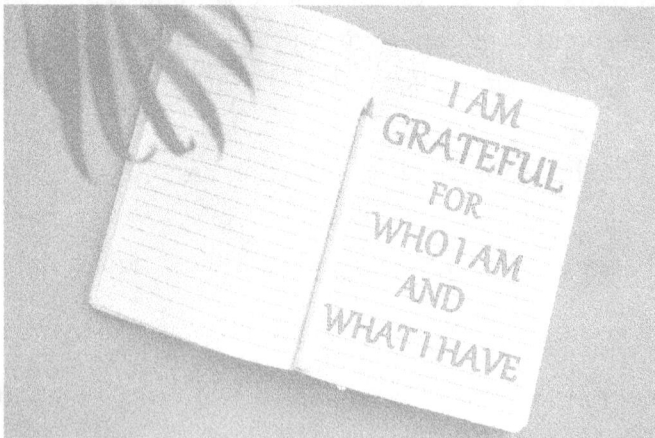

Take a moment to check in with yourself:

- What am I grateful for today? My supportive family, my health or my body's ability to carry me through each day?

- What work opportunities am I thankful for? A fulfilling career, a great team or a new project that challenges and excites me?

- What resources do I have that I appreciate? My ability to work remotely, access to tools that help me perform at my best or a mentor guiding me along my journey?

- How have past challenges helped me grow, both personally and professionally?

These prompts are designed to connect gratitude to both your personal and work life, creating a holistic sense of appreciation.

Step 7: Visualise Success

Visualisation is a technique often used by top performers to mentally rehearse success. Before stepping into your office or joining a virtual meeting, take a moment to visualise yourself confidently moving through your day. Picture yourself speaking clearly, handling tasks efficiently and interacting with colleagues effortlessly. This practice doesn't just boost confidence; it also primes your brain to recognise and seize opportunities for success. From a cognitive neuropsychological perspective, visualisation taps into the brain's ability to rewire neural pathways, much like how physical activities such as yoga or tai chi support neuroplasticity.

By mentally rehearsing your success, you are not just imagining a better day – you are preparing your mind to make it a reality. Use this mental tool to envision yourself thriving, grounded and strong throughout your workday.

Here are some reflective questions to guide your visualisation:

- What does success mean to me today, in both my personal and professional life? Is it completing tasks efficiently, building meaningful connections or maintaining a work-life balance?

- How does my definition of success align with my values? Am I honouring integrity, creativity, compassion or resilience as I move through my day?

- What will it feel like to achieve my goals today? Will I feel a sense of accomplishment, ease or fulfilment in work and personal interactions?

By engaging in this reflective visualisation, you prepare your mind and body to approach your day with clarity and strength, setting the stage for success.

Step 8: Grounding Techniques

Grounding is about bringing your awareness back to the present moment, helping you stay focused and calm no matter what is happening around you. Its techniques like deep breathing, body scanning and mindfulness exercises that can be instrumental to centre yourself and reduce stress during a busy workday. This is important for maintaining emotional regulation, especially when your nervous system is under pressure. Tapping into these techniques connects directly to polyvagal theory, as they help you access the vagal brake – bringing your body into a state of calm and safety. Whether it is a few mindful breaths or a short stretch at your desk, grounding will make it easier to navigate the ups and downs of your day with grace.

Step 9: Empower Yourself

Finally, remember that you have everything you need within you to succeed today. Empowerment comes from recognising your resilience and strength. The practices we have explored throughout this book – from mindful movement to breathwork and from sleep optimisation to nutrition – are all about building a solid foundation of well-being. When you feel good in your body, your mind follows suit, leaving you better equipped to handle whatever challenges come your way.

As you step into your workday, know that these practices support you and that you have the power to shape your experience with intention, focus and presence. This isn't just about surviving the day. These practices help you thrive with confidence and joy. It is also important to pay attention to how you talk to yourself. Your mind can sometimes become a barrier, preventing you from letting go and truly feeling.

Take a moment to listen to your internal conversations. Are you nurturing yourself or holding yourself back? Remember, you are your own leader and guide. Once you realise this, you can relinquish external expectations and empower yourself with trust, compassion and self-acceptance.

Here are some positive affirmations to inspire and uplift you:

- I trust in my abilities and the strength within me.

- I embrace challenges as opportunities for growth.

- I am worthy of success and happiness in my life.

- I speak to myself with kindness and compassion.

- I have the power to create my path and make meaningful choices.

- I am resilient and can navigate whatever comes my way with grace.

- My well-being is a priority, and I honour my needs.

- I choose to focus on the positive and celebrate my achievements, no matter how small.

Repeat these affirmations to yourself throughout the day, allowing their positive energy to resonate within you as you move forward with confidence and purpose.

As you move forward with the practices outlined in this chapter, remember that how you begin your workday is more than just about getting things done – you are showing up with purpose, clarity and presence. One of the most powerful lessons is recognising how you speak to yourself. Our inner dialogue can be our greatest ally or worst enemy, shaping how we approach challenges, handle stress and connect with others. Nurturing a kind, supportive relationship with yourself is key to navigating the ups and downs of work and life with resilience. Equally important is being mindful of the company you keep and the information you consume. The people you surround yourself with, the books you read, the shows you watch and the voices you listen to all contribute to the narrative that feeds your perceptions and beliefs. These inputs help create your reality, so choose them with care. Your mind is your most powerful asset, capable of shaping how you feel and thrive in your work and personal life.

As you embrace authenticity, set intentions, release negativity and encourage gratitude, know that each small action contributes to a bigger picture – a workday and a life filled with confidence, presence and joy. It is a constant learning journey, but with every step, you will find yourself more connected, grounded and ready to meet whatever the day brings.

Take, for example, my client Ravi, a highly successful professional who frequently travels internationally for work. Each morning, he incorporates some of these techniques into his routine, helping him stay centred and ease into the day. For Ravi, meditation initially started as a form of self-care, a way to ground himself amidst the demands of his career and the disruptions of constant travel. Over time, it evolved into something much more – he now writes and records his meditations, crafting unique reflections that empower him and others. This proactive approach boosts his productivity and also strengthens his emotional resilience. What a wonderful way to tap into creativity, deepen self-awareness and share that calm energy with those around him.

For those who travel frequently or face similar challenges, these techniques are simple and can be adapted to fit your lifestyle. I learned this on my journey when I achieved a consistent morning routine. I started with small changes – five to ten minutes of breathwork and a few stretches each morning. Over time, I embraced a more structured routine that sets a positive tone for my workday. As someone who works from home, I have noticed a significant improvement in managing stress and staying focused.

If you are a parent working from home with small children or a frequent traveller for work, you can still carve out time for these practices. It might mean waking up a little earlier or adjusting your routine based on your schedule, but the benefits are worth it. Each moment you invest in nurturing your well-being adds up, creating a foundation from which you can confidently and joyfully approach your work and personal life.

As we close this chapter, I encourage you to reflect on your mornings and consider how to integrate these practices into your daily life. Embrace the journey, honour your unique path and remember that you have the power to shape your experience with intention and authenticity. The ripple effects of these small, consistent actions will guide you toward a fulfilling and resilient workday.

Key Points

- **The power of a morning routine.** A consistent morning routine can transform how you approach your day, grounding you in calm, focus and resilience. By starting the day with mindful practices, you create a foundation that supports productivity and well-being, no matter the challenges ahead.

- **Aligning with intention and authenticity.** Setting intentions each morning aligns your actions with your values, helping you show up as your true self in work and life. Authenticity and intentionality allow you to navigate interactions meaningfully and develop stronger, more positive connections.

- **Using grounding techniques to manage stress.** Simple grounding practices – such as deep breathing, stretching and gratitude – help you stay centred in high-pressure situations. By calming the nervous system, these techniques improve your ability to respond thoughtfully rather than impulsively, creating a ripple effect that positively impacts your interactions and work environment.

- **The benefits of embracing flexibility and neuroplasticity.** As you consistently practise mindful techniques, you reduce stress and enhance your brain's flexibility and neuroplasticity. This adaptability helps your mind respond to challenges more easily, reinforcing emotional resilience and long-term mental well-being.

- Creating a supportive inner dialogue. How you speak to yourself can shape your day and your approach to challenges. Nurturing a kind, empowering inner dialogue builds confidence and resilience, helping you move through your workday with self-compassion and positivity.

- **Empowering your journey with reflection and creativity.** Personalise your morning routine by incorporating reflection, creativity and gratitude. Journaling, creating a vision board or visualising success adds depth to your practice, allowing you to create a more meaningful and inspiring start to each day, tailored to your unique journey and goals.

Chapter 11
Professional Development and Career Growth

"The biggest mistake that you can make is to believe that you are working for somebody else. Job security is gone. The driving force of a career must come from the individual. Remember: Jobs are owned by the company, you own your career!"
– Earl Nightingale

Professional development and career growth have taken on new dimensions in today's ever-evolving work landscape, especially for those of us working from home. With the increasing flexibility of remote work, the traditional nine-to-five office job is no longer a constraint. Instead, this shift opens up a world of growth, learning and even entrepreneurship possibilities.

What exactly do I mean by professional development? Professional development is acquiring new skills, knowledge and insights that empower you to advance in your career. This journey involves recognising opportunities, setting goals and taking actionable steps to elevate your position and expertise or explore new paths like venturing into entrepreneurship. However, it is important to understand that the path to professional growth is rarely linear. It requires a mix of curiosity, adaptability and resilience. Professional development is essential for career success because it keeps you competitive in an ever-changing environment. When working remotely, getting comfortable and neglecting your personal growth can be easy. If you don't take the time to focus on learning and expanding your skill set, you might miss out on valuable opportunities, and your skills could quickly become outdated.

This is where mindful goal-setting comes into play. Establishing clear and measurable goals creates a roadmap for your development. Consider how your goals align with your values and aspirations. This connection will help keep you motivated and engaged, mainly when challenges arise. Remember, communication is key as you pursue your goals. In addition, creating a strong network can provide invaluable insights and support, further enhancing your professional growth.

The beauty of remote work is that it allows you the flexibility to tailor your development to suit your unique circumstances and aspirations. Yet, as you embark on this journey, keeping your nervous system in mind is important. We often get swept up in the hustle, leading to overwhelm. Recognise that not everything requires your energy.

Practise distributing your energy mindfully. You might have less to give on some days than others, which is perfectly okay. Being attuned to your emotional state allows you to maintain a balanced perspective as you progress and to recognise when it is time to pause, reflect and take time for yourself.

As you build your skill set, start steadily. Forming consistent habits is vital; think of them as non-negotiable commitments to your growth. You are not just developing skills, you are creating a system that works for you. Hold yourself accountable, track your progress and celebrate small wins. And remember, while feedback from others can be helpful, never seek external validation.

Be your own source of approval. Nurture self-compassion and take time to acknowledge your efforts along the way. If this feels challenging at times, remember that it is okay to give yourself permission to feel valued, proud and accomplished. After all, you are the one doing the work – be humble and be proud!

In this chapter, we will explore how to identify opportunities for career development in a remote setting, venture into entrepreneurship and emphasise the importance of personal development in shaping your future success. Through inspiring client stories and practical advice, you will gain valuable insights into embracing remote work for your professional growth. You will also learn how to navigate the challenges of entrepreneurship with confidence and resilience. Remember, your career is a journey, not a destination. Each step you take towards professional development is an investment in yourself.

Embrace the flexibility of remote work as an opportunity to learn, grow and adapt. Committing to your own growth will enhance your skills and pave the way for new possibilities and a fulfilling career path.

"At every job, you should either learn or earn. Either is fine. Both are best. But if it's neither, quit."
– Garry Tan

Each new skill you acquire has the potential to open doors to unexpected opportunities and directions. Stay consistent in your efforts, yet remember to be patient and compassionate with yourself along the way. Building these habits is a journey in itself. So, embrace the process, trusting that every step forward, however small, contributes meaningfully to your evolving path.

Steps to Harness the Opportunities Effectively

For working professionals, harnessing opportunities for growth is essential in navigating an ever-evolving career landscape. By taking proactive steps to develop new skills, set clear goals and create structured plans, you can establish a career that meets industry demands and aligns with your personal passions and aspirations.

As much as these steps serve as a roadmap, they empower you to approach challenges confidently, build resilience and encourage continuous self-improvement. Ultimately, embracing this journey offers the potential for heightened job satisfaction, expanded career possibilities and a fulfilling path that reflects both professional ambition and personal values.

Step 1: Identify Opportunities for Growth

The first step on your professional development journey is to reflect deeply. This isn't just a fleeting moment of thought. This is a deliberate process where you ask yourself vital questions about your career. What skills do you currently possess? What skills are required in your industry that you might be lacking? This introspective journey is important for uncovering areas where you can grow.

Take a moment to consider:

- What tasks do you find challenging or outside your comfort zone?

  These challenges often point to skills that would greatly benefit you. If you find public speaking daunting, for instance, honing this skill could open new doors for you.

- Are there industry certifications or qualifications that would improve your career prospects?

  Research what qualifications are valued in your field. There may be a certification in project management or digital marketing that could elevate your profile.

- What hobbies or interests could translate into professional skills?

Think about the skills you have developed outside of work. Are you a whiz at graphic design? That could translate beautifully into a new aspect of your professional role.

Consider how you might relate to individuals like Paul, a successful international businessman who discovered his passion for singing after a serious health crisis. What began as a simple hobby became a transformative outlet for him. While managing a demanding career, Paul embraced his love for music, gradually integrating it into his life. This provided him with a creative expression and honed his vocal skills. By reflecting on his interests and weaving his passion for singing into his professional narrative, Paul carved out a unique niche for himself, which led to new opportunities and collaborations. Ultimately, he turned his love for singing into a successful career alongside his full-time job, demonstrating that pursuing your passions can lead to unexpected and rewarding pathways in your personal and professional life.

"If you want to conquer fear, don't sit at home and think about it.
Go out and get busy."
– Dale Carnegie

When thinking about your future, consider what skills and knowledge you might need if you decide to start a new business. This could be something part-time alongside your current job or a complete transition. Are there entrepreneurial skills you need to develop, such as financial literacy, marketing strategies or networking abilities? Take small, actionable steps toward acquiring these skills.

As you embark on this reflective journey, keep in mind that growth often requires stepping outside your comfort zone. By identifying opportunities for development, you are not just preparing for your next role. You are setting the stage for a fulfilling and enriched career path.

If some of these skills feel challenging or off-putting, consider understanding how and why they are important. Then, if they still don't feel like the right fit, think about delegating them to a professional. This is an investment in your business. While you focus on your strengths and use them to grow your business, you can collaborate with experts in areas that aren't your speciality. Building this support network complements your abilities and strengthens your venture as a whole.

Step 2: Set Clear and Measurable Goals

Once you have a clearer understanding of your growth areas, the next step is to set specific, measurable goals. Think of clear goals as a beacon illuminating your path toward desired outcomes. Well-defined objectives make it easier to stay focused and motivated.

Take a moment to reflect:

- What specific skill or knowledge do you want to acquire in the next three months?

    Reflect on areas that excite you. Is there a particular skill that keeps calling your name? Maybe you have always wanted to explore data analytics or improve your negotiation tactics. Setting your sights on a tangible goal can give you direction and purpose.

- How will you measure your progress?

  Consider what success looks like for you. Will it be through completing an online course, earning a certification or successfully launching a project? Visualising your end goal can help you create a roadmap to get there. You could track your progress in a journal or set up check-ins with a mentor to keep you accountable.

- What potential roadblocks do you foresee, and how can you prepare to address them?

  Life can throw curveballs, and it is helpful to anticipate challenges before they arise. Are you worried about finding the time to study or fearing that you might not grasp a new concept? Identifying these hurdles can help you develop strategies to overcome them. For instance, scheduling regular study blocks in your calendar or seeking support from a peer could make a significant difference.

- Which tasks do you find particularly challenging or outside your comfort zone?

  These difficulties often highlight areas where skill development is highly beneficial. For instance, if managing complex projects feels overwhelming, developing your organisational and prioritisation skills could make these tasks more manageable and enhance your overall effectiveness.

- Are there certifications or specialised training programmes that could enhance career prospects?

  Look into credentials that are valued in your industry. For example, acquiring a certification in data analysis or business communication might broaden your skill set and make you a more competitive candidate for future roles.

- What hobbies or personal interests could contribute to your professional skill set?

  Consider the abilities you have honed outside of work. Are you a passionate photographer or a skilled writer in your spare time? These talents could seamlessly complement your current role or open doors to new responsibilities. Recognising these connections might inspire you to weave your passions into your career path.

You might ask yourself: What skills and knowledge do you need to start a new business part-time alongside your current job or as you transition into something new altogether? It could involve learning about digital marketing, understanding financial management for small businesses, building a supportive network or even seeking mentorship.

Networking can connect you with like-minded individuals and potential collaborators, while mentorship offers guidance from those with relevant experience. Additionally, consider which tasks might be best delegated to professionals – areas like accounting or specialised marketing strategies. Being specific about your goals and outlining clear steps, including when to seek support, will empower you to approach your new venture with confidence and focus.

Setting clear and actionable goals motivates and clarifies your path forward. With a defined destination, every step you take gains meaning and intention. Remember, your goals should genuinely reflect your aspirations and align with your values, passions and long-term vision. Embrace this journey as continual growth. Each milestone is a meaningful accomplishment, building momentum and confidence as you progress. Celebrate these moments, knowing they are part of a bigger picture that leads to a fulfilling and purpose-driven career.

Step 3: Create a Plan of Action

Now that you have set your goals, it is time to develop a concrete action plan. Consider this plan your personal roadmap – it provides structure and direction, helping you stay committed to your professional development.

Take a moment to consider:

- How can you integrate professional development into your weekly schedule?

  Think about your current commitments and where you might carve out time for learning or networking. For example, could you allocate a few hours on a Saturday morning to start a new online courshappe? You could also dedicate your lunch breaks to connecting with industry peers during the week. Mapping out specific time slots makes it easier to commit.

- What specific resources can support your learning?

Consider the tools you have. Have you read books that have inspired you, or are there online courses that align with your goals? A workshop could provide valuable insights. Taking the time to curate these resources can significantly boost your learning experience.

- How will you hold yourself accountable to this plan?

    Accountability is a game-changer. How will you track your progress? Can you share your goals with a trusted friend or colleague who can check in with you? You might also find value in journaling your experiences. Reflecting on what you have learned and the steps you have taken can reinforce your commitment.

Let us relate this to the story of Paul. While managing his demanding job, Paul realised he needed a structured approach to attend to this newfound passion. Paul began to set aside time each week for vocal training and songwriting, meticulously planning his practice sessions around his work commitments. By integrating these practices into his routine, he transformed his hobby into a flourishing side career, illustrating the power of a well-crafted plan. Remember, a well-structured plan acts as your roadmap, ensuring you stay focused on your objectives.

Consistency is key – small, daily actions can compound into significant progress over time. As you create your plan, ask yourself what skills and knowledge are essential if you want to start a new business part-time or transition into a new career altogether. This reflection can guide you in identifying the areas you need to focus on. By acknowledging these requirements and committing to your action plan, you set the stage for success.

Step 4: Track Your Progress and Adapt

Regularly tracking your progress is important for staying on course in your professional development journey. However, adaptability is just as important; remain open to modifying your approach. After all, the path of growth is rarely linear, and flexibility can often lead to new insights and opportunities.

Take a moment to reflect:

- How will you assess your progress?

    Will you check in weekly, monthly or quarterly? Setting specific review times can help you stay accountable and allow you to celebrate small wins along the way.

- What metrics or indicators will help you evaluate your success?

    Consider what success means to you personally. Are there particular goals you can use to track your progress, such as gaining a certification, expanding your client base or mastering a new skill? Defining these markers will help you stay aligned with your vision and focused on what truly matters.

- Have you noticed patterns or obstacles that require you to adjust your plan?

Reflecting on your experiences can reveal valuable insights. Are there recurring challenges that hinder your progress? Perhaps time management is an issue, or you find specific skills more challenging. Recognising these patterns allows you to adapt your strategy and stay aligned with your goals.

Remember that tracking your progress offers valuable insights into what's effective and may need adjustment. Embrace the flexibility to refine your strategy – this adaptability is a strength, not a setback, and each thoughtful adjustment can bring you closer to your goals. As you reflect on your journey, consider the skills and knowledge that could support a part-time business or a complete career shift.

This awareness empowers you to seek the right resources, connect with supportive networks, and stay aligned with your growth. Trust in this process, knowing that each step, whether forward or adjusted, is a meaningful part of your evolving path.

Step 5: Network and Seek Mentorship

In remote work, many professionals discover the freedom and flexibility that can spark entrepreneurial ambitions. Networking remains vital in any professional landscape, but it is important when working remotely. Just because you are not in a physical office doesn't mean you should isolate yourself. In fact, remote work offers unique opportunities to connect with individuals from around the globe.

Take a moment to reflect:

- Who in your network can support your goals?

  Think about family, friends, former colleagues or acquaintances who have skills or insights that align with your aspirations. Reaching out to them can lead to valuable conversations.

- What virtual events, webinars or online communities can you join to expand your professional circle?

  Consider joining virtual conferences, industry panels or networking sessions hosted by organisations in your field. You might also explore online communities, professional discussion groups or virtual coworking spaces that facilitate meaningful connections and knowledge sharing with like-minded professionals. These spaces can provide valuable opportunities to expand your network and stay engaged in industry developments.

- How can you leverage social media platforms to engage with industry peers?

  Social media can be a powerful tool for networking. Consider joining industry-specific groups or participating in discussions to boost your visibility and develop relationships.

- Who inspires you: writers, researchers or academics?

  While they may seem unreachable due to their expertise and authority in the field, remember that they are humans, too. Many are open to communication and willing to provide guidance. Don't hesitate to contact them – they may appreciate your initiative and offer valuable insights.

Imagine yourself considering a side business while balancing a full-time job. The flexibility of remote work offers a unique opportunity to explore your passions without the immediate pressures of a full-time commitment. With this flexibility, you can test ideas, plan thoughtfully and learn at your own pace, all while maintaining a stable income.

As you embark on this journey, remember the value of understanding others before sharing your perspective. Be humble; you are learning. By actively listening, you open doors to growth and insight, which can be especially valuable in the early stages of building a new venture. This approach strengthens connections and broadens your understanding of various viewpoints, helping shape your business approach in a way that resonates with you and others. As you gain more confidence and recognise the significance of your presence, you will naturally find yourself engaging more purposefully. This self-assurance can lead to deeper, more authentic connections and help you build a strong professional network. Embracing these practices allows you to grow a fulfilling side business enriched by the meaningful relationships and insights you gather along the way.

The financial aspects of entrepreneurship can feel daunting, but there are practical steps you can take to navigate this path with confidence. Begin by seeking out business planning and financial management resources to build a strong foundation. Consulting with financial advisors or mentors can also provide personalised guidance tailored to your needs, offering insights that can prevent costly missteps.

Additionally, consider building up your expertise by pursuing relevant certifications or skills that will add credibility to your chosen field. If finances are tight, think creatively; you may be able to barter your existing skills in exchange for mentorship, guidance or even services that support your business. This approach can open doors to valuable learning opportunities without straining your budget.

The flexibility of remote work allows you to grow your business gradually and at a pace that aligns with your goals. This scalability means you can experiment, refine strategies and respond to feedback, all without the immediate pressure of a full-time commitment. By embracing this thoughtful, incremental approach, you can build a venture that aligns with your values and aspirations. Remember, entrepreneurship is a journey, and taking small, intentional steps can create a foundation for lasting success.

Step 6: Overcome Challenges and Obstacles

Entrepreneurship, especially when juggling it with remote work, comes with its own challenges. Yet, every obstacle can also be an opportunity for growth. You may have struggled with time management and balancing your full-time job while managing a side business or personal project. Financial planning can be overwhelming, especially when you have other responsibilities, like caring for family members or managing household tasks. These hurdles can be daunting but can also pave the way for resilience and adaptability.

Take a moment to reflect on your journey:

- What specific challenges have you faced professionally, and how have they shaped your outlook?

    Consider the hurdles you have encountered – whether they be time management, balancing multiple responsibilities or navigating workplace dynamics. Reflect on how these experiences have influenced your perspectives and values. Have they made you more resilient? Do they inspire you to pursue your passions more fervently? Understanding your challenges can provide valuable insights into your growth and help you identify areas you want to improve. Feel free to journal your thoughts and insights; you can always revisit them for reflection.

- Are there tools or techniques that might help you manage your time and resources more effectively?

    Think about the methods you currently use and evaluate their effectiveness. Are you employing time blocking, prioritising tasks or using digital tools to stay organised? Research new techniques or resources that would improve your productivity. These might include apps for project management, mindfulness practices to reduce overwhelm, or scheduling regular breaks to maintain focus and energy. The right tools can empower you to make the most of your time and help you balance your professional aspirations and personal well-being.

222

- When setbacks arise, what strategies can you employ to maintain your motivation and keep pushing forward?

  It is natural to face obstacles, but how you respond to them can determine your trajectory. Reflect on the practices that help you regain your motivation during tough times. This could be leaning on your support network, engaging in self-care activities or revisiting your goals to realign your focus. Consider journaling your thoughts, practising gratitude or visualising your success to reinforce your determination. By endorsing resilience, you will navigate challenges more effectively and emerge from them stronger and more capable.

Common struggles like managing time, planning finances and balancing personal commitments can be particularly challenging for those working from home. However, these obstacles can become manageable with a clear plan, realistic goals and a flexible mindset. Remember that progress matters more than perfection; each challenge is an opportunity to learn and grow, building resilience.

To support your journey, consider researching industry trends, pursuing courses aligned with your interests or connecting with mentors for guidance and perspective. Embrace the idea that challenges are essential to growth. Each challenge gives you valuable wisdom and knowledge, creating space to reflect, adapt and develop. By viewing obstacles as stepping stones, you bring on mental flexibility, adaptability and self-confidence, empowering you to navigate your career and life with purpose and positivity.

The Key to Professional Growth

At the heart of both professional development and entrepreneurship is personal growth. Remote work offers a unique opportunity to elevate your skills while investing in your inner development. Take Ravi, for example. As a frequent traveller for his job, he realised that nurturing his personal growth was essential for maintaining clarity, focus and productivity.

By establishing a morning routine with mindfulness practices and physical activity, he stays grounded and balanced, even amidst the demands of his busy schedule. Embracing habits such as mindfulness, healthy routines and self-awareness is important. These practices support your professional ambitions and contribute to your overall well-being. Whether you are aiming for a promotion, launching a side business or simply seeking greater satisfaction in your work, personal development forms the foundation that empowers you to navigate the challenges and triumphs of your career journey with resilience and clarity – enabling you to show up each day with purpose and intention.

Remote work offers distinctive professional and personal growth avenues, allowing you to harness flexibility to your advantage. As you identify growth opportunities, explore entrepreneurship or concentrate on self-improvement, remember that the remote work model empowers you to take control of your career path. Embrace your curiosity, remain committed to your goals and recognise that challenges are integral to the process.

As you consider your personal development journey, reflect on the skills and knowledge you need to embark on a new business venture, whether a part-time pursuit alongside your current job or a complete career change or entrepreneurship. What expertise do you need to acquire? Can courses, mentors or resources help you bridge the gap? Answering these questions will clarify your path and equip you for the journey ahead.

With the right mindset, clear intentions and a willingness to step outside your comfort zone, you can thrive in the remote work landscape while achieving personal and professional success. Whether through skill-building, networking or taking that leap into entrepreneurship, your growth is firmly in your hands – and the possibilities are endless. Remember, every step you take toward self-improvement fuels your journey, opening doors to new opportunities and helping you create a fulfilling and successful career. Embrace this personal development journey, and let it guide you toward achieving your aspirations.

"Your talent determines what you can do. Your motivation determines how much you are willing to do. Your attitude determines how well you do it."
– Lou Holtz

Key Points

- **Embrace continuous learning and growth.** Professional development involves acquiring new skills and knowledge to stay competitive in a dynamic work environment. Committing to continuous growth enhances adaptability, ensuring a fulfilling and resilient career.

- **Set clear and measurable goals.** Mindful goal-setting provides direction and motivation, creating a roadmap for your career journey. Clear, measurable objectives help you stay focused and accountable, making each step towards your goals more intentional and impactful.

- **Harness the flexibility of remote work.** Remote work offers unique opportunities to personalise professional development and even explore entrepreneurship. By leveraging this flexibility, you can build a career that aligns with your passions and personal aspirations, creating a balanced, purpose-driven path.

- **Develop a supportive network and seek mentorship.** Networking remains crucial, especially in remote settings, as it offers insights, support and growth opportunities. Building connections with mentors and industry peers enriches your perspective, strengthens your journey, and boosts your professional potential.

- **Build resilience and adaptability in the face of challenges.** Every obstacle encountered is a chance to grow, fostering resilience and adaptability. By viewing challenges as learning opportunities, you empower yourself to confidently navigate setbacks and emerge stronger in your career and personal life.

- **Prioritise personal development as a foundation for success.** Investing in personal growth through habits like mindfulness and self-care enhances professional effectiveness and well-being. By nurturing personal and professional growth, you create a balanced approach that fuels your journey toward a rewarding and successful career.

Chapter 12
Remote Team Management: Creativity, Innovation and Crisis Management

"No one can whistle a symphony. It takes an orchestra to play it."
– H.E. Luccock

In today's world of remote work, managing a team goes beyond assigning tasks – it requires developing and maintaining connection, resilience and creativity across distance. The shift from traditional office settings to remote and hybrid work models has fundamentally changed the dynamics of teamwork and leadership. With geographical separation and limited face-to-face interaction, remote leaders encounter distinct challenges and significant opportunities.

Remote team management, especially for those adapting to this new landscape, involves more than just overseeing tasks – it requires establishing an environment where open communication, innovation and a sense of shared purpose can thrive, even across screens. Leadership in this context involves investing in personal growth, adaptability and self-awareness. As a leader, you will notice that your state of mind and energy directly impact team morale and performance. The demands of remote leadership call for a deeper connection to your own goals and the needs of your team, creating a work culture where everyone feels engaged, motivated and empowered to contribute their best.

Navigating Remote Leadership with Authenticity

True leadership, especially in remote settings, is grounded in authenticity. Leaders aren't just project managers; they are mentors, motivators and anchors for their teams. Your self-awareness and emotional balance set the tone for your team's cohesion and productivity.

There are days that come when you may feel stretched thin. It could result from a sleepless night, the stress of managing multiple tasks or simply an "off" day. Your team picks up on this energy. But your team looks to you for guidance and clarity even during these times. Being honest about these moments builds trust. When you share that you have had a sleepless night but are present for the team, you show vulnerability that strengthens connection and mutual respect. This sincerity helps your team see you as relatable and genuine, creating a culture where people feel supported and valued.

It is important to note that authenticity in leadership isn't about revealing every challenge you face. It is about modelling resilience in a way that results in psychological safety, allowing your team to feel comfortable bringing their authentic selves to work. As my friend Stuart says, "Don't worry about mowing the lawn when crocodiles are biting your ass."

Leaders who are out of touch with themselves often avoid addressing challenging issues, redirecting focus to less critical tasks to evade discomfort. This lack of self-awareness can breed team frustration, confusion and disconnect. Remote leadership requires heightened responsibility to stay grounded in purpose, creating a growth-focused culture that supports resilience and connection. By focusing on what matters most, leaders establish an environment where innovation thrives and every team member feels secure and empowered to contribute to a shared vision.

Real Challenges in Remote Leadership

Managing a remote team presents a unique set of challenges that require trust, compassion, accountability and flexibility – qualities that may feel unfamiliar to leaders accustomed to in-office oversight. The shift to remote work has left companies divided. While some embrace it as a forward-looking model, others remain sceptical, especially those with experience in leadership rooted in traditional office culture. These leaders may question productivity levels or fear losing spontaneous collaboration and direct oversight. This generational gap in work philosophies can create tension, as younger employees often prioritise autonomy, flexibility and a results-focused culture, while senior leaders may still associate productivity with visible presence and fixed hours.

To bridge this divide, it is essential to maintain open dialogue and respect differing perspectives, shifting focus from physical presence to tangible results. Setting clear, transparent metrics that emphasise project milestones and the quality of outcomes helps align expectations. This approach provides clarity for senior leaders who may be cautious about remote setups, showing them that remote work can drive productivity without constant oversight. Regular, results-based reporting also reassures stakeholders and maintains accountability, while clear communication around goals and outcomes minimises misunderstandings and ensures that everyone has a shared vision of success. Ultimately, remote work requires a balanced approach to flexibility and structure and an openness to new ways of measuring and celebrating team achievements.

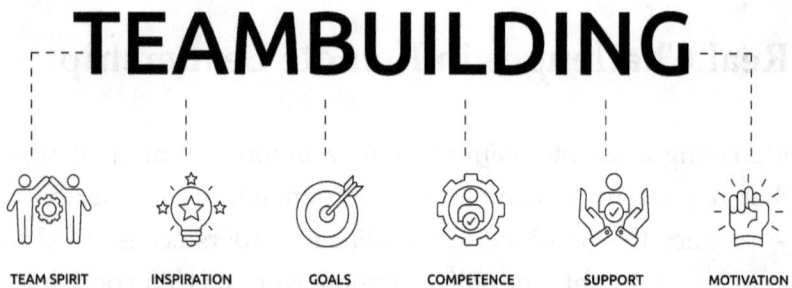

TEAMBUILDING

| TEAM SPIRIT | INSPIRATION | GOALS | COMPETENCE | SUPPORT | MOTIVATION |

Practical Strategies for Effective Remote Team Management

Leading a remote team goes beyond ensuring technical efficiency and meeting deadlines. It is about developing a culture prioritising connection, trust and adaptability – especially as AI and other technological shifts transform today's workplace. As employees face the need to upskill and adapt to these changes, they may respond in different ways. Some may embrace the chance to work with AI, while others feel uncertain and concerned about the impact of automation on their roles. Leaders are called to balance technological adaptation with genuine support and encouragement in this evolving landscape, helping each team member confidently navigate these shifts.

This section offers actionable strategies for building a culture where collaboration, creativity and resilience thrive. Leaders can invest in a supportive environment by maintaining open lines of communication, encouraging innovation, addressing challenges proactively and respecting each team member's unique needs and strengths. By prioritising these elements, remote team leaders can create a resilient, cohesive team ready to excel together, no matter the distance or demands of a dynamic work environment. Each step provides a framework for nurturing individual and collective growth, ensuring that remote teams succeed and find fulfilment in the journey. Remember, as a leader, you play a pivotal role in shaping the team's cohesion and culture. It begins with you taking a holistic approach – understanding the whole system and recognising that group synergy starts with your leadership.

Encourage Open Communication and Connection

In the absence of in-person meetings, building an atmosphere of trust and open communication is vital because it is the foundation for effective collaboration, team cohesion and overall productivity. When people work remotely, they miss out on many non-verbal cues and spontaneous conversations that often help reinforce understanding, connection and transparency in an office setting. Trust and open communication replace these in-person dynamics, ensuring team members feel comfortable sharing ideas, asking questions and addressing challenges proactively. Without them, remote teams are at risk of isolation, miscommunication, reduced collaboration and heightened stress. Team members may feel disconnected and disengaged, unsure of where they fit within the team, which can diminish their motivation over time. Without an open dialogue, misunderstandings go unresolved, leading to mistakes, duplicated efforts or even conflicts.

This atmosphere stifles creativity and collaboration, as team members may hesitate to share ideas or feedback. Without the support of a transparent culture, individuals might manage challenges alone, increasing stress and potential burnout.

In other words, with trust and open communication, teams experience stronger productivity, heightened accountability and a unified drive toward shared goals. When team members feel secure and valued, they are more likely to engage fully, collaborate freely and contribute ideas without hesitation. This foundation of trust encourages proactive problem-solving, reduces misunderstandings and contributes to a supportive environment where challenges are met collectively. In turn, the team's sense of purpose and connection grows, creating a resilient, motivated group capable of achieving their highest potential together.

Take, for instance, a team member facing a heavy workload at home while also managing family responsibilities. Without an informal support system like hallway conversations, they might feel isolated. Regular check-ins give them a platform to voice their challenges, helping to reduce feelings of stress and isolation. These simple practices create a culture of connection, reminding team members they are part of a supportive network. Remember, you are not just leading a team—you are looking after and nurturing all these nervous systems, including your own.

One of my clients, for instance, implemented bi-weekly well-being chats, creating a space where team members could discuss work updates and share personal experiences and challenges. These sessions helped deepen connections and even sparked friendships among team members, helping them feel more supported and valued. This regular rhythm of informal check-ins provided more than just project alignment. It offered a source of compassion and genuine listening, both essential for mental and emotional well-being in a remote setting.

As a leader, these interactions allow you to observe the group's dynamics and build upon the positive interplay, further strengthening team cohesion and trust. Leadership, after all, is a well-rounded approach that requires balancing strategic goals with human connection, ensuring that both the tasks and the people behind them are nurtured and supported.

Prompt Questions

- How can I create a safe, judgment-free environment where my team feels comfortable sharing professional and personal challenges?

  Reflect on practices, like regular check-ins or informal video calls, that could develop openness and trust within your team.

- Am I providing enough opportunities for informal connection that bridge the gap created by distance?

  Consider whether adding these opportunities could help bridge the distance and build a stronger sense of connection and community.

- If a team member opens up about personal challenges, am I prepared to respond compassionately and, if necessary, guide them toward additional resources?

  Reflect on how you can be a supportive, empathetic leader while respecting boundaries and confidentiality within the team.

Encourage Creativity and Innovation

Remote work provides freedom from traditional office routines, opening up opportunities for creative initiatives like "idea-sharing Fridays" or "passion project hours," where team members can present fresh ideas and share personal interests. These sessions often spark inspiration, with one person's insights offering valuable takeaways for others. For instance, a team member passionate about sustainability might introduce eco-friendly practices, benefiting the company and inspiring colleagues.

Encouraging innovation also means empowering team members to take ownership of their work, which increases productivity and morale. Allowing flexibility in work hours – such as parents balancing home responsibilities or individuals who perform best outside traditional hours – helps each person find their rhythm, ultimately benefiting team output. Leaders endorse trust and respect by setting clear goals while allowing flexibility in how they are achieved. This flexibility is crucial during periods of crisis or unexpected challenges, where resilience and adaptability become key. A team that views setbacks as opportunities to learn and innovate can navigate pressures with creativity and confidence, ensuring long-term success.

Prompt Questions

- What specific initiatives, like "idea-sharing Fridays," can I introduce to encourage my team to share new ideas?

  Reflect on activities that could foster a culture of creative thinking and make space for diverse ideas and perspectives.

- How am I empowering my team to take ownership of their work while allowing them the flexibility to find a rhythm that suits their individual needs?

  Consider whether you are offering team members enough autonomy to manage their work hours and tasks in a way that supports both their creativity and productivity.

- How can I support a resilient culture that embraces flexibility and adaptability without losing focus on our goals?

  Consider ways to provide guidance while encouraging your team to approach changes and crises with a creative, solutions-focused attitude.

Welcome Crisis Management With Resilience and Compassion

Crises are an inevitable test of a team's resilience. Preparing them to handle unexpected challenges with clarity and composure is essential. Leaders who approach these moments with compassion reinforce their team's adaptability. Establishing clear crisis protocols, defining roles and ensuring access to essential resources can provide the structure needed to face challenges effectively. During the pandemic, many teams benefited from weekly check-ins that combined project updates with emotional support, helping maintain focus while forming a sense of security.

Recognising that stress affects everyone differently, leaders can help prevent burnout by encouraging mental health days and offering wellness resources. Simple reminders – like "Your well-being matters" – emphasise that self-care is valued, not just productivity. When team members face personal crises, having protocols in place allows others to adjust workloads temporarily, offering flexibility without pressure. This compassionate approach reassures team members that they are supported, building resilience and motivation, even in challenging times.

It is just as important to check in with yourself during a crisis. While your team relies on you to lead with clarity and strength, carrying the weight of everything on your shoulders can quickly become overwhelming. Take time to look after your well-being. Reach out to a mentor, coach or trusted friend for support – a space where you can recharge and share concerns without judgment. This self-care isn't only beneficial for your team; it is essential for your well-being as well.

When you are grounded and supported, you can lead with resilience, compassion and clarity, avoiding burnout and staying fully present for whatever comes your way.

As leaders, we often need to rely on ourselves to push through challenging times. Many may find it difficult to ask for help, seeing vulnerability as a weakness. It is common to think, *"How can I be vulnerable as a leader? That would make me look weak."* But remember, self-care as a leader isn't a luxury but a necessity. Recognising when to seek support is a strength, not a shortcoming. Being honest with yourself and acknowledging your needs allows you to show up authentically and set an example for your team. This openness prioritises your well-being and encourages a culture of support and resilience.

Throughout this book are strategies to strengthen your resilience. Remember, vulnerability isn't a weakness; it's a form of self-awareness that helps you recognise when to pause, listen to your body and create space to breathe and process. These techniques can benefit not only you but also your team, reinforcing a culture of authenticity and care. Leading with openness and compassion creates an environment where others feel empowered to grow. This kind of leadership has a lasting impact: a resilient team that is connected, adaptable and ready to thrive together.

Prompt Questions

- What protocols and resources do I currently have to support my team during a crisis, and are they accessible and clear to everyone?

  Consider if there are gaps in communication or resources that could be improved to help your team feel prepared and supported in unexpected situations.

- Am I encouraging a compassionate approach to crisis management by offering flexibility, mental health days and wellness support during challenging times?

  Think about how you can integrate supportive practices that help prevent burnout and reinforce a balanced approach to work and well-being.

- How can I create space in my routine to regularly check in with myself and seek support when needed, ensuring I stay grounded and present for my team?

  This question encourages you to reflect on your self-care practices and consider practical ways to maintain your well-being and resilience, ultimately benefiting your leadership and team dynamics.

Tailor Your Management to Individual Needs

Each team member brings unique skills, personalities and work habits. In a remote setting, that can either enrich the team dynamic or introduce friction, depending on how it is managed. As a leader, recognising and adapting to each person's strengths, challenges and preferred working style is essential for building a cohesive and supportive team. Meanwhile, leveraging these strengths adds meaningful value to the company, team projects and overall goals.

Some people thrive with structured tasks, while others excel in more flexible, autonomous roles; adjusting your management style to suit these differences creates a sense of inclusion and respect. For instance, a team member who feels uncomfortable speaking in large meetings may prefer contributing through written feedback or smaller group discussions.

This adaptability extends to understanding personal circumstances, such as balancing work with family obligations. Flexibility in these areas promotes shared understanding, reducing stress and strengthening team cohesion. A client once shared that when one of her team members struggled with family care responsibilities, adjusting timelines and goals eased the pressure, reinforcing support and trust within the team.

A personalised approach empowers each team member to engage in ways that align with their strengths and comfort zones, helping them reach their full potential while contributing to a resilient, unified team.

Prompt Questions

- How well do I understand each team member's unique working style, strengths and personal circumstances?

  Reflect on whether you have taken time to learn about each individual's preferences and challenges, and consider how this knowledge could shape your management approach.

- How can I develop a culture where individual strengths are recognised and supported, helping people reach their potential?

  Reflect on how you can create a team dynamic that values diverse working styles and empowers each member to bring their best to the table.

- Am I providing a variety of ways for team members to contribute, considering that some may prefer written feedback or smaller discussions over larger meetings?

  Think about how offering different modes of participation could help create an inclusive environment where everyone feels comfortable and engaged.

Addressing Company Resistance and Building a Culture of Growth

Some companies remain hesitant about fully embracing remote work. They voice concerns about productivity, team cohesion and the long-term sustainability of remote setups. Balancing these concerns with the needs of a remote team can be a delicate task for leaders, requiring a thoughtful, outcome-oriented approach. Success stories and measurable results are essential tools for bridging this gap. Regularly highlighting your team's accomplishments and demonstrating how remote work contributes to these achievements can shift perspectives, reinforcing that productivity and collaboration are not limited to physical office spaces.

To address resistance effectively, it is also important to recognise and bridge generational divides in attitudes toward remote work. Senior staff members, who may have built their careers on in-office presence, might equate physical visibility with productivity. Aligning these differing views starts with transparency and clear communication, focusing on an outcomes-based model. This approach shows how prioritising results, rather than hours spent in a specific location, can meet productivity goals and support employee well-being. Demonstrating that accountability and trust are the foundation of remote team success helps reassure those sceptical of non-traditional work setups.

Workshops and seminars can also play a valuable role in bridging this gap, offering insights into the benefits of remote work and addressing common concerns. Consider inviting senior team members to share their expertise and experience through seminars or mentorship roles. Senior staff can mentor remote employees, sharing insights on productivity, discipline and effective communication, which helps preserve institutional knowledge and build a sense of continuity. Integrating senior voices helps strengthen a culture of learning and respect, showing that remote work is an adaptable model that values input from all experience levels.

By emphasising outcomes, encouraging transparency and leveraging the insights of senior staff, you can help build a culture that adapts to remote work and thrives within it. This will encourage growth, collaboration and resilience across your team.

Prompt Questions

- How can I use success stories and measurable outcomes to address company concerns and highlight the effectiveness of remote work?

  This question prompts you to consider how sharing your team's achievements can demonstrate the value of remote work and help shift perspectives within the organisation.

- What steps can I take to bridge generational divides in attitudes toward remote work, and how can senior staff contribute to building a culture of growth and respect?

  This question encourages you to explore ways to address differing perspectives within the company and leverage the experience of senior staff to foster a supportive, inclusive culture.

Commitment and Passion as Foundations of Remote Leadership

Effective leadership is more than a title or a set of responsibilities. It is your commitment to growth, resilience and authenticity. At its core, leadership is your ability to guide, inspire and bring out the best in others while staying connected to a clear purpose. This commitment is essential in a remote environment, where the absence of physical presence means you must rely on trust, communication and a clear sense of direction to keep your team engaged and motivated.

True leadership goes beyond managing tasks; it is about embodying the values you want to see within your team, creating a culture of accountability, creativity and genuine connection.

A strong sense of purpose is fundamental to effective leadership. When you are connected to your purpose, you bring energy, passion and clarity that influences the entire team. Without this connection, your motivation can wane and small obstacles can become major roadblocks. If you are disconnected from your purpose, you might find yourself avoiding real issues and focusing instead on minor tasks to sidestep challenges – or even projecting your insecurities onto the team.

This behaviour creates inefficiencies and breeds frustration within your team, as members sense a lack of direction and become uncertain of their roles. Over time, this can lead to your team doubting your leadership skills and questioning your decisions. They may even begin to feel resentment towards you, creating their narratives behind your back, which further erodes trust and cohesion. This disconnect damages morale and creates a toxic undercurrent that hinders your team's ability to work cohesively toward shared goals.

In contrast, you inspire confidence and trust when you fuel your team with empowering energy and clarity. Your leadership presence is felt even when you are not physically there, as your guidance and influence resonate throughout the team. This creates an environment of mutual respect, shared purpose and a sense of security that allows your team to thrive, regardless of the challenges they face.

For you as a leader, professional and personal growth are intertwined and essential to developing the resilience needed in a remote setting. Professional growth involves continuously learning new skills, refining leadership techniques and staying adaptable in an ever-evolving workplace. This growth helps you respond to challenges, make informed decisions and guide your team effectively.

On the other hand, personal growth is about self-reflection, emotional intelligence and a deep commitment to self-awareness. It involves understanding your motivations, values and areas for improvement, enabling you to lead with authenticity and compassion. As a leader, you are not only responsible for guiding others but also for leading yourself. Your ability to inspire and support your team is directly tied to your inner strength and resilience. People will test you, circumstances will challenge you and stress will inevitably creep in. Your investment in your well-being is crucial; it is the foundation that allows you to handle pressures with clarity and composure.

By prioritising self-care, maintaining your physical health and cultivating mental resilience, you set a powerful example and ensure that you have the energy and focus to meet the demands of leadership.

Committing to personal and professional growth is also about setting a standard for your team. When you actively pursue growth, you model the behaviours you want to see in others: curiosity, adaptability and resilience. This inspires your team to invest in their development, creating a culture where continuous learning and self-improvement are valued and encouraged. Your willingness to grow demonstrates that leadership is a journey, not a destination. Every challenge offers an opportunity for deeper insight and greater resilience. Leading remotely intensifies these dynamics, requiring an extra level of resilience from you.

Every challenge you encounter – from managing team dynamics across distances to navigating external pressures – tests your character and resolve. Rather than seeing these challenges as setbacks, embrace them as opportunities for personal and professional growth. Remote leadership requires adaptability and the ability to balance structure with flexibility. By staying connected to your purpose, you fortify your motivation and create a stable, inspiring presence that your team can rely on, even when faced with uncertainty.

Read the autobiographies of highly successful people, follow them on social media, watch their documentaries, or, if possible, have a conversation with them. You will see a common thread: They *never* stop growing. They simply don't. There is always a new project, book, or class.

I have had the privilege of meeting individuals who are now in their 70s and 80s, people who have – without exaggeration – contributed to world history, driven innovation and shaped global progress through their dedication and vision. These individuals remain some of the *most* coachable and open people I have met. Despite their age and all they have achieved, they have *never* stopped learning. Listening to their stories fires me up, and I feel deeply humbled and grateful to have been able to learn from such remarkable minds. Their commitment to growth is a powerful reminder that continuous learning is the ultimate path to excellence.

In summary, leadership in a remote environment requires a continuous commitment to growth, self-reflection and a strong connection to purpose. This approach keeps you grounded, resilient and prepared to face challenges confidently. When you embrace these qualities, you foster an environment of trust and mutual respect, building a team that is productive, motivated, engaged and empowered to contribute its best.

Prompt questions

- How connected do you feel to your purpose as a leader, and how does this purpose show up in your daily interactions with your team?

  This question encourages you to reflect on your core motivations as a leader and helps you evaluate whether your actions and presence align with the values you want to embody within your team.

- What specific steps are you taking to invest in your personal and professional growth, and how are they reflected in your leadership style?

This question prompts you to examine your growth strategies and consider how continuous learning and self-improvement shape your leadership and influence your team.

- How do you balance the structure of remote leadership with the flexibility needed to adapt to challenges and individual needs?

This question challenges you to evaluate your approach to maintaining balance in a remote setting, ensuring that you stay resilient, adaptable and able to support the team's goals and individual well-being.

- What legacy of growth and curiosity are you creating within your team, and how can you model a mindset of continuous learning?

This question invites you to think about the long-term impact of your leadership and how your commitment to learning inspires a culture of curiosity and growth within your team.

In remote leadership, your commitment to growth, purpose and authenticity is the foundation of your effectiveness. Leading from a distance requires a deeper connection to your purpose and the ability to ensure your presence is deeply felt, even when you are not physically there. This demands an unwavering dedication to continuous learning and growth – not just for the success and cohesion of your team but for your fulfilment and resilience as a leader.

When your leadership is rooted in purpose and authenticity, your guidance resonates through your actions, words and the culture you cultivate, empowering your team to thrive regardless of physical distance. Leadership in this context demands more than overseeing tasks; it calls for setting a standard of integrity, adaptability and trust, creating a culture where every team member feels motivated and valued.

As a leader, you are not only responsible for guiding others but also for leading yourself. Each challenge and change tests your character and resilience, offering a choice: to see obstacles as setbacks or as opportunities for growth.

Embracing these experiences, rather than shying away, strengthens your connection to purpose, fuels your motivation and builds a stable presence that inspires your team even in times of uncertainty. By investing in your development, you model the same curiosity, adaptability and commitment you want to see within your team, creating a lasting legacy of continuous improvement.

Effective remote leadership is a journey of self-reflection, growth and connection. Building a cohesive team starts with you. When you embrace the challenges of remote work with courage and purpose, you invest in a supportive, resilient environment that goes beyond productivity. You develop a team culture of trust, mutual respect and a shared commitment to excellence.

As you lead with passion and integrity, you empower your team to bring their best every day, inspired to contribute meaningfully to a shared vision.

Key Points

- **Purpose-driven leadership.** Staying connected to your purpose as a leader is essential in a remote setting, where physical distance requires you to lead with clarity and motivation. When grounded in purpose, you bring energy and focus that inspires your team to stay engaged and aligned with shared goals.

- **Balancing structure with flexibility.** Remote leadership requires adaptability, balancing structured oversight with the flexibility to support individual needs and challenges. Setting clear expectations yet allowing flexibility creates an environment that fosters accountability and personal well-being.

- **Continuous growth and self-reflection.** Effective leadership is a constant learning and self-improvement journey, where personal and professional growth are deeply intertwined. By actively pursuing growth and reflecting on your motivations and areas for improvement, you model resilience and curiosity for your team.

- **Self-care as a leadership essential.** Leading others starts with leading yourself and prioritising your well-being and resilience. By investing in self-care, you sustain the mental and emotional strength necessary to handle challenges with composure, setting a powerful example for your team.

- **Creating a culture of learning and accountability.** Your commitment to growth sets a standard for the team, encouraging a culture where continuous learning and accountability are valued. When you model curiosity and adaptability, you encourage team members to embrace challenges and pursue their development, creating a motivated and resilient team.

- **Embracing challenges as opportunities.** Every challenge in remote leadership tests your character and resilience, offering opportunities for deeper insight and growth. By viewing obstacles as pathways to improvement, you strengthen your connection to purpose and demonstrate that true leadership is about embracing growth, not just managing tasks.

"Success is not how high you have climbed, but how you make a positive difference to the world."
– Roy T. Bennett

Chapter 13
Future Trends and Reflection

"I am not afraid of storms, for I am learning how to sail my ship."
– Louisa May Alcott

Looking toward the future of remote work, we are clearly moving beyond simple productivity gains to an approach that values personal well-being, cultural diversity and technological innovation. This evolution isn't just about "getting things done" from afar; it is about creating a work culture that is more inclusive, dynamic and human-centred. A major force shaping this landscape is the rise of AI.

On one hand, AI tools can automate repetitive tasks, speed up decision-making and create more personalised workflows, which gives people space to focus on meaningful, creative projects. On the other hand, AI also brings challenges, such as concerns over job displacement and the need to upskill constantly. Today's workforce must adapt to a landscape where skills like compassion, creativity and critical thinking – skills AI can't replicate – are highly valued. Alongside AI, the push for flexibility, globalisation and a stronger sense of community is redefining what remote work can be. These shifts open doors to building deeper connections, gaining fresh perspectives and encouraging both personal and professional growth in ways traditional office environments couldn't. Remote work is no longer just about where we work. It is about how we connect, collaborate and innovate.

For companies, embracing remote work as a long-term approach unlocks new opportunities, such as accessing a global talent pool and building multicultural teams with diverse perspectives. This diversity fuels creativity and innovation as team members bring new viewpoints and ideas that disrupt conventional thinking. However, managing a global team comes with unique challenges like navigating different time zones, bridging cultural gaps and ensuring employees feel connected rather than isolated.

Companies that succeed in this space are the ones investing in a supportive, inclusive culture tailored to remote teams. For example, wellness programmes explicitly geared toward remote employees, virtual seminars on stress management and regular team-building activities can help maintain trust and connection. Supporting the well-being of remote teams channels a workplace into a space where employees feel empowered to bring their best ideas forward.

For remote workers, globalisation and flexibility offer incredible opportunities. Collaborating with clients, colleagues and mentors from around the world broadens horizons and enriches learning experiences. Imagine a freelance designer working with clients across countries, as each new project brings fresh ideas and cultural insights that keep their work vibrant and relevant. This global exposure transforms remote work into a bridge to new perspectives and growth. However, flexibility and globalisation have their challenges, too. Remote work can sometimes feel isolating, especially without the daily interactions and community of an office environment.

Moreover, with the rapid pace of tech and tool updates, keeping up can feel daunting, potentially leading to disconnection or burnout. That is why adaptability and openness to change are no longer simple nice-to-haves. They are essential. Maintaining curiosity, building a strong support network and creating meaningful, connection-focused conversations rather than only task-oriented meetings can help remote workers stay grounded and engaged.

This chapter will explore these future trends and how they shape professional development and well-being. Understanding these trends is important for adapting to the dynamic nature of remote work. Without this awareness, we risk missing out on the very elements that make remote work fulfilling and sustainable. Therefore, creating a sense of community and being open to learning and adapting to new practices and technologies is essential.

The Dual Nature of Remote Work: Benefits and Challenges

One of the greatest appeals of remote work is undoubtedly its flexibility. Setting your own hours, designing a personalised workspace and weaving in family life or personal pursuits create a new work-life harmony. Studies have shown that this flexibility can boost productivity, job satisfaction and well-being.[1] By allowing team members to shape their schedules, companies invite fresh creativity and innovation. Flexibility becomes more than just a perk; it catalyses empowerment, letting employees feel more in control of their work lives.

With freedom comes the challenge of balance. Many remote workers find it difficult to "switch off," leading to an "always on" mindset that can lead to burnout. Without the natural boundaries of a physical office, it is easy for work to extend into personal time. This is where the practices from earlier chapters – like mindfulness, sleep routines and regular movement – become invaluable. Mindful breaks and structured routines can help us draw boundaries, resist the lure of constant availability and re-establish a healthy balance.

Remote work can be as isolating as much as it is empowering. Humans are social beings. Regular connection is key to staying resilient against the isolation remote work sometimes brings. Quick messages with a colleague or virtual coffee hours can remind us that we are part of something bigger, creating a sense of belonging and easing the mental load of working independently.

Still, mindfulness, in particular, is a recurring theme because it is a simple yet powerful tool for remote work. A few mindful breaths, a walk or even a moment of stillness can help you pause and reset, bringing clarity and grounding when work feels overwhelming. Mindfulness reminds us to respect our time and energy; over time, it becomes integral to a sustainable remote work routine.

In the end, remote work's flexibility is its strength and challenge. Without clear boundaries, this freedom can lead to stress. Integrating practices like mindfulness, community connection, movement and routine can help establish a balanced approach that supports productivity and well-being. The journey to finding balance in remote work doesn't happen overnight, but with small, intentional changes, each day can feel more purposeful and fulfilling.

Creating a Culture of Support

As remote work becomes more permanent, companies have to do more than just allow flexibility. They need to create a culture that actively supports productivity and overall well-being. This means moving beyond surface-level policies to invest in an environment where remote employees can thrive. Creating policies that support both productivity and holistic wellness is essential. One practical way to support well-being is through regular virtual check-ins where team members can share challenges and successes. These sessions help bridge the gap created by physical distance, offering employees a space to voice concerns and feel part of a shared purpose. In-person group trips or retreats can also be highly impactful, giving the team a chance to bond, relax and enjoy a change of scenery.

Another effective approach is organising seminars on stress management or hosting performance enhancement workshops.

For example, a client of mine recently invited his team from Japan to visit the UK. While some time had been dedicated to work and on-site experience at the company, the trip also included cultural visits, local excursions and social gatherings to deepen connections. This blend of professional and cultural exchange strengthens collaboration and a shared sense of adventure and unity that can enhance team cohesion long after the trip ends.

Embracing an understanding of polyvagal theory within the workplace can elevate these efforts further. By recognising how our nervous systems respond to stress, leaders can foster psychologically safe environments where remote employees feel emotionally connected and supported, even from a distance. For example, a tech start-up client set up a weekly virtual coffee hour. Simple as it was, this gathering allowed team members to share updates and connect outside of work projects. What started as a modest experiment became a grounding part of their week, providing a space where everyone's voices and experiences felt acknowledged.

On a broader level, companies need to recognise the importance of rest and recovery – topics we explored in earlier chapters on sleep, movement and mindfulness. The demands of remote work can make it difficult for employees to switch off, so companies should actively promote healthy work-life boundaries. By encouraging breaks, promoting movement and integrating wellness into the workday, organisations clearly communicate that well-being is a priority.

Incorporating mindfulness into team settings can also create grounding moments. Starting or ending a meeting with a mindful breath or quick check-in helps reduce stress and create a supportive atmosphere. In addition to emotional support, providing ergonomic resources – like stipends for home office setups – can comfort and prevent the physical strains accompanying home-based work. Offering resources or guidance on ergonomic setups signals that the company values its employees' long-term health and productivity.

All these elements – psychological safety, community-building, clear boundaries, mindfulness and ergonomic support – create a sustainable and fulfilling remote work culture. The most successful remote teams are those in which employees feel seen, valued, respected and supported in ways that encourage productivity and personal well-being.

Creating such a culture isn't a one-off policy change. It requires ongoing commitment and the willingness to adapt as new needs arise. When employees feel genuinely supported, their motivation, creativity and loyalty flourish, benefiting the organisation.

In today's evolving landscape of remote work, these principles help transform the potential challenges of distance into opportunities for connection, growth and resilience. A holistic approach boosts individual well-being and strengthens the company, paving the way for sustainable engagement and community.

Crafting a Personal Roadmap for the Future

Each chapter in this book provides insights into how working professionals can establish a balanced, fulfilling work life, even within the ever-evolving landscape of remote work. While remote work can bring challenges, it also offers an incredible opportunity to integrate wellness practices into daily life in ways that traditional offices may not have allowed. However, achieving this balance takes intentionality, self-awareness and a roadmap where well-being is prioritised.

Remote work can sometimes make it tempting to be "always available" or, conversely, can lead to isolation. By embracing a holistic approach to wellness, you can create a foundation for resilience, growth and empowerment. Take, for example, our discussions on mindful daily routines. Working remotely allows you to design your day around your energy, focus and well-being. Prioritising quality sleep, setting boundaries and allowing moments for movement aren't just lifestyle choices – they are essential tools for thriving in this new world of work.

Creating a personal roadmap for remote work is ultimately about taking small, intentional steps. You might start by beginning your day with a grounding ritual, scheduling regular breaks or setting specific times to unplug. These small acts of self-care add up to create a work life that is more balanced, enriching and sustainable.

For instance, Chapter 3 emphasised how regular movement sharpens the mind and promotes clarity, while Chapter 5 illustrated how quality rest fuels resilience. By bringing these practices into your daily life, you nurture your health and equip yourself with the strength to face challenges and succeed professionally.

Looking ahead, the future of remote work holds both exciting opportunities and inevitable challenges. Organisations and individuals alike have a role to play in shaping this landscape. While companies must build structures that support well-being, we are also responsible for prioritising self-care and continuous growth. Remote work invites us to rethink how we connect, collaborate and care for ourselves and others. It is an opportunity to create a productive work life rich with meaning, connection and joy.

As you move forward, ask yourself: *Am I taking time to pause and reflect? Am I setting boundaries that truly support my well-being? Am I creating a workspace that allows for creativity, calm and focus?* These aren't just questions – they are signposts guiding you toward a balanced and fulfilling work life. In a constantly evolving world, these moments of reflection serve as a compass, helping you make choices that promote both productivity and peace.

By embracing these principles, we contribute to a more connected, innovative and resilient professional community. It is in such a community where we can all thrive together. Let us take these learnings forward and build work environments where well-being is prioritised, creativity is celebrated, and each of us can find meaning and fulfilment in our work. As you continue this journey, may these insights remind you that your work life can be as enriching, harmonious and vibrant as you choose to make it, with each intentional choice leading you toward a future filled with growth, connection and lasting satisfaction.

Above all, remember to approach this journey with curiosity and openness. Befriend your nervous system, listen to its guidance, be coachable and show up in your authenticity. Doing so will create a fulfilling work life for yourself and inspire those around you to pursue the same.

Key Points

- **Future trends in remote work.** Embrace globalisation and flexibility. Remote work is evolving beyond productivity gains, blending well-being, cultural diversity and technological innovation. By embracing these trends, companies can tap into a global talent pool, encouraging multicultural collaboration and infusing creativity and innovation into remote teams.

- **Balancing freedom and structure in remote work.** Remote work offers unparalleled flexibility. It enhances creativity and job satisfaction but can also cause burnout by blurring the lines between work and personal life. Integrating mindful practices, intentional routines and regular breaks allows remote workers to invest in a more balanced, sustainable work environment where productivity and personal well-being coexist.

- **Building a culture of support for remote workers.** For organisations, encouraging a supportive remote work culture means prioritising productivity and well-being. Regular virtual check-ins, wellness programmes and community-building initiatives allow remote employees to feel valued and connected, strengthening team cohesion and engagement across distances.

- **Creating psychological safety and connection in remote teams.** Psychological safety and social connection are essential for remote teams. By establishing spaces where employees feel emotionally supported – through initiatives like virtual coffee hours and open feedback channels – organisations can reduce isolation and build a resilient sense of belonging.

- **Mindful practices as a path to preventing burnout.** Mindfulness, intentional breaks, sleep hygiene, nutrition and movement are vital tools for managing remote work demands and preventing an "always-on" mentality. Simple practices like breath awareness, mindful movement and periodic pauses aid focus, renewal and a balanced approach to maintaining personal boundaries.

- **Crafting a personal roadmap for well-being and success.** Small, intentional actions – like setting clear boundaries, incorporating mindful movement and prioritising rest – can support productivity and well-being. This roadmap is a holistic guide, ensuring a remote work experience that encourages professional growth and personal fulfilment.

"Time is the coin of your life. It is the only coin you have, only you can determine how it will be spent."
– Carl Sandburg

Conclusion

As we close this journey, let us revisit the essential pillars explored in this book. Each pillar forms the intricate framework that can transform your work life and well-being.

We began with insights into designing an ergonomic workspace, recognising the importance of physical comfort as a foundation for productivity and longevity in any work setting. This extended into a broader exploration of movement, integrating mindful physical activity into our day to prevent physical strain and contribute to mental clarity and emotional resilience.

With chapters on polyvagal theory and mindfulness, we uncovered the deep interconnections between our physiological states and daily stress responses, showing how small, mindful practices can shift our nervous system toward a state of safety, focus and playfulness. We also explored sleep quality and its profound effect on mental and physical performance, drawing attention to simple yet powerful routines that ensure rest and recovery – especially important in remote work environments where the boundaries between work and rest can blur.

Chapters on nutrition and the holistic kitchen introduced a mindful approach to eating, connecting what we consume with our mental well-being, mood stability and productivity. Nutritional habits were shown to be more than personal choices; they are foundational to our resilience and capacity to tackle each day. With goal setting, we explored aligning personal and professional aspirations, laying out a sustainable path to success. Meanwhile, professional development and career growth chapters provide frameworks to advance in today's dynamic work landscape, empowering you to move forward with clarity and intention.

For those leading teams, especially in remote settings, our discussions on team management, creativity and crisis management provided a practical guide to encouraging innovation while managing stress and well-being – not only for yourself but also those you guide. Finally, reflecting on future trends, we zoomed out to consider the ongoing transformations in the workplace and the relevance of adaptability, agility and continuous learning.

The Bigger Picture

These insights reveal a deeper understanding of the complex relationship between our physical, mental and emotional states, especially in an ever-evolving professional landscape. The traditional "work-life balance" has transformed into a more integrated model where wellness, productivity and growth are intertwined. This book's holistic approach emphasises that thriving in work and life isn't about compartmentalising these areas but recognising the interconnectedness that allows each element to reinforce the others.

Our work culture is in transition, and professionals must now be adaptable, resilient and equipped with tools to manage both external demands and internal states. In this context, the practices shared here empower you to respond, adapt and thrive, creating a ripple effect in your life and the lives of those around you. This journey is not just about professional success but about finding harmony within oneself and contributing to sustainable growth in your career and beyond.

Final Thoughts & Next Steps

If there is one idea to carry forward, it is this: Intentionality and awareness can reshape your relationship with work, health and fulfilment. This inner alignment becomes your strongest asset in a world filled with external demands. By embracing the practices of mindful movement, nutrition, restful sleep and play, you create a reservoir of resilience and vitality that you can tap into, no matter the external pressures. This book isn't merely a guide but an invitation to create a life where productivity and personal well-being coexist harmoniously.

The journey doesn't end here. As a next step, I encourage you to revisit these chapters and experiment with applying their principles in your life. Small, consistent adjustments often yield the most significant results. To help you stay inspired, I offer free guided visualisations and downloadable files accessible via the QR code provided.

Download Resource

For those looking to deepen their understanding, my upcoming online course provides a structured, step-by-step approach to integrating these tools into your daily life. Additionally, you are welcome to contact me about my seminars and life coaching programme through my website, mindlabcoaching.com, where we can work together to apply these insights even more fully.

Whether exploring these resources or implementing one simple change, each step brings you closer to a balanced, vibrant and productive work life. Here is to the next chapter of your journey – one marked by growth, resilience and a deeper connection to yourself. Trust the process, and enjoy the journey!

References

Introduction

[1] American Psychological Association. (2022) *Stress in America™ 2022: The State of Our Nation*. [Online]. Available at: [https://www.apa.org/news/press/releases/stress/2022/concerned-future-inflation].

[2] DeFilippis, E., Impink, S. M., Singell, M., Polzer, J. T., and Sadun, R. (2020) 'Collaborating during Coronavirus: The impact of COVID-19 on the nature of work', *National Bureau of Economic Research*. [Online]. Available at: [https://www.nber.org/system/files/working_papers/w27612/w27612.pdf].

[3] World Health Organization. (2024) *Mental health and well-being at the workplace: Protection and inclusion in challenging times*. Geneva: WHO.

Chapter 1

[1] Knapp, M. L. and Hall, J. A. (2010) *Nonverbal Communication in Human Interaction*. 7th edn. Boston, MA: Wadsworth,

Cengage Learning, pp. 176–176.

[2] Field, T. (2010) 'Touch for socioemotional and physical well-being: A review', *Developmental Review*, 30(4), pp. 367–383. doi:10.1016/j.dr.2011.01.001.

[3] Romney, C. E., Smith, J., and Doe, A. (2023) 'Hugs and cortisol awakening response the next day: An ecological momentary assessment study', *International Journal of Environmental Research and Public Health*, 20(7), p. 5340. doi:10.3390/ijerph20075340.

[4] Hölzel, B. K., Lazar, S. W., and Gard, T. (2011) 'How does mindfulness meditation work? Proposing mechanisms of action from a conceptual and neural perspective', *Perspectives on Psychological Science*, 6(6), pp. 537–559. doi:10.1177/1745691611419671.

Chapter 2

[1] Russo, F., Ribeiro, P., and Lee, H. (2021) 'The effects of workplace interventions on low back pain in workers: A systematic review and meta-analysis', *International Journal of Environmental Research and Public Health*, 18(23), p. 12614. doi:10.3390/ijerph182312614.

[2] Gobbo, S., Martin, A., and White, K. (2019) 'Physical exercise is confirmed to reduce low back pain symptoms in office workers: A systematic review of the evidence to improve best practices in the workplace', *Journal of Functional Morphology and Kinesiology*, 4(3), p. 43. doi:10.3390/jfmk4030043.

[3] Du, T., Zhang, M., and Li, P. (2022) 'Computer and furniture affecting musculoskeletal problems and work performance in work-from-home during COVID-19 pandemic', *Journal of Occupational and Environmental Medicine*, 64(11), pp. 964–969. doi:10.1097/jom.0000000000002622.

[4] Cabegi de Barros, F., Moriguchi, C. S., and de Oliveira Sato, T. (2022) 'Effects of workstation adjustment to reduce postural exposure and perceived discomfort among office workers: A cluster randomized controlled trial', *Applied Ergonomics*, 102, p. 103738. doi:10.1016/j.apergo.2022.103738.

[5] Du, Zhang, and Li, 'Computer and furniture affecting musculoskeletal problems', p. 964.

[6] Nakatsuka, K., Tanaka, Y., and Ito, M. (2023) 'Association between pain intensity in the neck and components of a workstation: A cross-sectional study on Japanese office workers', *International Journal of Industrial Ergonomics*, 93, p. 103385. doi:10.1016/j.ergon.2022.103385.

[7] Gholami, M., Hassan, F., and Reza, K. (2022) 'Investigating the effect of keyboard distance on the posture and 3D moments of wrist and elbow joints among males using OpenSim', *Applied Bionics and Biomechanics*, 2022, pp. 1–10. doi:10.1155/2022/5751488.

[8] Morales-Bravo, J. and Navarrete-Hernandez, P. (2022) 'Enlightening wellbeing in the home: The impact of natural light design on perceived happiness and sadness in residential spaces', *Building and Environment*, 223, p. 109317. doi:10.1016/j.

buildenv.2022.109317.

Chapter 3

[1] Porges, S. W. (2001) 'The polyvagal theory: Phylogenetic substrates of a social nervous system', *International Journal of Psychophysiology*, 42(2), pp. 123–146. doi:10.1016/s0167-8760(01)00162-3.

[2] Dana, D. (2018) *The Polyvagal Theory in Therapy: Engaging the Rhythm of Regulation.* New York: W.W. Norton & Company, pp. 36–38.

[3] Porges, 'The polyvagal theory', pp. 123-146

[4] De Couck, M., Caers, R., and Schmitz, H. (2019) 'How breathing can help you make better decisions: Two studies on the effects of breathing patterns on heart rate variability and decision-making in business cases', *International Journal of Psychophysiology*, 139, pp. 1–9. doi:10.1016/j.ijpsycho.2019.02.011.

[5] Jerath, R., Edry, J., and Barnes, V. A. (2006) 'Physiology of long pranayamic breathing: Neural respiratory elements may provide a mechanism that explains how slow deep breathing shifts the autonomic nervous system', *Medical Hypotheses*, 67(3), pp. 566–571. doi:10.1016/j.mehy.2006.02.042.

[6] Field, 'Touch for socioemotional and physical well-being', pp. 367-383.

[7] Ross, A. and Thomas, S. (2010) 'The health benefits of yoga and exercise: A review of comparison studies', *The Journal of Alternative and Complementary Medicine*, 16(1), pp. 3–12. doi:10.1089/acm.2009.0044.

[8] Dana, *The Polyvagal Theory in Therapy*, pp. 182–183.

[9] Dana, D. (2020) *Polyvagal Exercises for Safety and Connection: 50 Client-Centered Practices.* New York, NY: W.W. Norton & Company, p. 23.

[10] Dana, *Polyvagal Exercises for Safety and Connection*, p. 25.

[11] Kabat-Zinn, J. (2003) 'Mindfulness-based interventions in context: Past, present, and future', *Clinical Psychology: Science and Practice*, 10(2), pp. 144–156. doi:10.1093/clipsy.bpg016.

Chapter 4

[1] Dana, D. (2022) *2-Day Workshop: Polyvagal Theory in Action. Creating Safety & Connection with Trauma Clients.* Copyright 2022 PESI, INC.

[2] Dana, *Polyvagal Exercises for Safety and Connection*, pp. 87-89.

Chapter 5

[1] Höpfner, J. and Keith, N. (2021) 'Goal missed, self hit: Goal-setting, goal-failure, and their affective, motivational, and behavioral consequences', *Frontiers in Psychology*, 12, doi:10.3389/fpsyg.2021.704790.

Chapter 6

[1] Grèzes, J., Erblang, M., Vilarem, E., Quiquempoix, M., Van Beers, P., Guillard, M., Sauvet, F., Mennella, R., & Rabat, A. (2021) ' Impact of total sleep deprivation and related mood changes on approach-avoidance decisions to threat-related facial displays', *Sleep*, 44(12). https://doi.org/10.1093/sleep/zsab186

[2] Garbarino, S., Lanteri, P., Bragazzi, N. L., Magnavita, N., & Scoditti, E. (2021) 'Role of sleep deprivation in immune-related disease risk and outcomes', *Communications Biology*, 4(1). https://doi.org/10.1038/s42003-021-02825-4

[3] Poggiogalle, E., Jamshed, H., & Peterson, C. M. (2018) 'Circadian regulation of glucose, lipid, and energy metabolism in humans', *Metabolism*, 84, 11–27. https://doi.org/10.1016/j.metabol.2017.11.017

[4] García, A., Angel, J. D., Borrani, J., Ramirez, C., & Valdez, P. (2021) 'Sleep deprivation effects on basic cognitive processes: which components of attention, working memory, and executive functions are more susceptible to the lack of sleep?' *Sleep science* (Sao Paulo, Brazil), 14(2), 107–118. https://doi.org/10.5935/1984-0063.20200049

Chapter 7

[1] Gerritsen, R.J. and Band, G.P. (2018a) 'Breath of life: The respiratory vagal stimulation model of contemplative activity', Frontiers in Human Neuroscience, 12. doi:10.3389/fnhum.2018.00397.

[2] Porges, S. W. (2007) 'The polyvagal perspective', *Biological Psychology*, 74(2), 116–143. https://doi.org/10.1016/j.biopsycho.2006.06.009

Chapter 8

[1] Gibson, J. (2019) 'Mindfulness, interoception, and the body: A contemporary perspective', *Frontiers in Psychology*, 10, doi:10.3389/fpsyg.2019.02012.

[2] Pilozzi, A., Carro, C., and Huang, X. (2020) 'Roles of β-endorphin in stress, behavior, neuroinflammation, and brain energy metabolism', *International Journal of Molecular Sciences*, 22(1), p. 338. doi:10.3390/ijms22010338.

[3] Northey, J. M., Cherry, M. G., and Pumpa, K. L. (2018) 'Exercise interventions for cognitive function in older adults: A systematic review with meta-analysis', *British Journal of Sports Medicine*, 52(3), pp. 154–160. doi:10.1136/bjsports-2017-098136.

[4] Proietti, S. S., Chiavarini, M., Iorio, F., Buratta, L., Pocetta, G., Carestia, R., Gobbetti, C., et al. (2024) 'The role of a mindful movement-based program (Movimento Biologico) in health promotion: results of a pre-post intervention study', *Frontiers in Public Health*, 12, https://doi.org/10.3389/fpubh.2024.1372660.

[5] Hölzel, B. K., Lazar, S. W., and Treadway, M. T. (2011) 'Mindfulness practice leads to increases in regional brain gray matter density', *Psychiatry Research: Neuroimaging*, 191(1), pp. 36–43. doi:10.1016/j.pscychresns.2010.08.006.

Chapter 9

[1] Porges, S. W. (2001) 'The polyvagal theory: Phylogenetic substrates of a social nervous system', *International Journal of Psychophysiology*, 42(2), pp. 123–146. doi:10.1016/s0167-8760(01)00162-3.

[2] Knezevic, E., Andric, N., and Radovanovic, P. (2023) 'The role of cortisol in chronic stress, neurodegenerative diseases, and psychological disorders', *Cells*, 12(23), p. 2726. doi:10.3390/cells12232726.

[3] Servushan, P. (2023) *The Gut-Brain Axis: Understanding the Link Between Gut Health and Mental Disorders*. [Preprint]. doi:10.31219/osf.io/pdtr2.

[4] Kristeller, J. L. (2019) 'Mindfulness-Based Eating Awareness Training (MB-EAT)', *Handbook of Mindfulness-Based Programmes*, pp. 191–203. doi:10.4324/9781315265438-16.

[5] Uvnäs-Moberg, K., Handlin, L., and Petersson, M. (2015) 'Self-soothing behaviors with particular reference to oxytocin release induced by non-noxious sensory stimulation', *Frontiers in Psychology*, 5, doi:10.3389/fpsyg.2014.01529.

[6] Jacques, A., Debras, C., and Blanc, M. (2019) 'The impact of sugar consumption on stress-driven, emotional, and addictive behaviors', *Neuroscience and Biobehavioral Reviews*, 103, pp. 178–199. doi:10.1016/j.neubiorev.2019.05.021.

[7] Devassy, J. G., Howe, P. R., and Wong, M. (2016) 'Omega-3 polyunsaturated fatty acids and oxylipins in neuroinflammation and management of Alzheimer disease', *Advances in Nutrition*, 7(5), pp. 905–916. doi:10.3945/an.116.012187.

[8] Welty, F. K. (2022) 'Omega-3 fatty acids and cognitive function', *Current Opinion in Lipidology*, 34(1), pp. 12–21. doi:10.1097/mol.0000000000000862.

[9] Riebl, S. K., & Davy, B. M. (2013) 'The hydration equation', *ACSM's Health & Fitness Journal*, 17(6), 21–28. https://doi.org/10.1249/fit.0b013e3182a9570f

[10] Cherpak, C. E. (2019, August 1) 'Mindful Eating: A review of how the Stress-Digestion-Mindfulness triad may modulate and improve gastrointestinal and digestive function', *Integrative Medicine*, 18(4). https://pmc.ncbi.nlm.nih.gov/articles/PMC7219460/

Chapter 13

[1] Indradewa, R., & Prasetio, A. A. (2023) 'The influence of flexible working arrangements and work-life balance on job satisfaction: A double-layered moderated mediation model', *Jurnal Ekonomi Dan Bisnis*, 26(2), 449–476. https://doi.org/10.24914/jeb.v26i2.9551

About the Author

Andreja Borin, MSc, is a polyvagal-informed life coach and sports injury and rehabilitation therapist dedicated to helping individuals reconnect with their physical and mental well-being. Currently a psychology doctoral candidate, Andreja brings a scientific approach and compassionate understanding to her work, informed by years of experience in the wellness industry. Her own path to healing has profoundly shaped her development as a wellness practitioner. She understands that not all injuries leave visible scars; some of the deepest wounds lie within. This realisation has fuelled her commitment to supporting others in their life's pursuits, whether they face personal, physical or mental health challenges.

In her private practice, Andreja works with clients from all walks of life, from office professionals and athletes to individuals simply seeking a healthier, more fulfilling life. Her holistic approach draws from various therapeutic techniques informed by psychology and physiology studies and her pursuit of knowledge in cutting-edge fields like Polyvagal Theory. She recognises that health and resilience require a deep connection and understanding of body, mind and spirit and uses this awareness to empower clients to build strength from within.

Beyond her practice, Andreja offers resources such as guided visualisations and coaching exercises, which can be found within her book, inviting readers to explore deeper aspects of their personal development. She also provides a life coaching programme for those seeking a more tailored experience in their unique journeys. With a focus on empowering others and nurturing genuine well-being, her work embodies a commitment to health that is both professional and deeply personal. She remains a devoted partner to her clients, helping them rediscover their potential and lead a balanced, fulfilling life.

*9 7 8 1 0 6 8 3 6 5 9 0 4 *